How to Win
Government Contracts

How to Win Government Contracts

Robert B. Greenly

VNR VAN NOSTRAND REINHOLD COMPANY

New York

Copyright © 1983 by Van Nostrand Reinhold Company Inc.

Library of Congress Catalog Card Number: 82-21859
ISBN: 0-442-23265-9

Manufactured in the United States of America

Published by Van Nostrand Reinhold Company Inc.
135 West 50th Street
New York, New York 10020

Van Nostrand Reinhold Company Limited
Molly Millars Lane
Wokingham, Berkshire RG11 2PY, England

Van Nostrand Reinhold
480 Latrobe Street
Melbourne, Victoria 3000, Australia

Macmillan of Canada
Division of Gage Publishing Limited
164 Commander Boulevard
Agincourt, Ontario M1S, 3C7, Canada

15 14 13 12 11 10 9 8 7 6 5 4 3 2

Library of Congress Cataloging in Publication Data

Greenly, Robert B.
    How to win government contracts.

    Includes index.
    1. Proposal writing in public contracting. I. Title.
HD3860.G73   1983   658.8   82-21859
ISBN 0-442-23265-9

Preface

How to Win Government Contracts shows you step-by-step how to get on the customer's qualified bidders' lists, how to determine your proposal budget, how to organize your proposal team, how to organize and write your proposal, and how to develop the crucial win strategy. It distills the experience of several hundred proposal efforts. Proposal writers who read and absorb what is presented will discover many ideas that can be applied immediately. The book will help you do your job better and improve your win/loss record. And, unlike consultants, *How to Win Government Contracts* won't leave when your proposal is finished. It's here to be used again and again.

Contents

Preface   v

1. Introduction   1
2. The Strategic Business Plan — Where It All Starts   16
3. Business Intelligence — Getting Competitor/Customer
   Information and Using It   23
4. The All-Important Preproposal Effort   30
5. The Proposal Effort   50
6. Writing the Winning Technical Volume   62
7. Writing the Winning Management Volume   70
8. Writing the Winning Logistics Support Volume   87
9. Preparing the Winning Cost Volume   95
10. The Critical Red Team Process for Proposal Review   106
11. Putting It All Together   112
12. The Postproposal Effort   143
13. Negotiations   160
14. How to Win International Contracts   170

Appendix A: Proposal Writer's Dictionary of Acronyms,
            Initialisms, and Abbreviations   176
Appendix B: Proposal Editor's Marks   191
Appendix C: Latin Reference Terms   192
Appendix D: Two-Letter State Abbreviations   193
Appendix E: A Few "Good Writing" References   194
Index   195

How to Win
Government Contracts

1
Introduction

- What is a proposal?
- What does a proposal contain?
- The proposal manager and his role?
- How long does it take to write a proposal?
- What events take place during the preparation of a proposal?

How to Win Government Contracts is packed solidly with strategies for winning government contracts, business planning strategies, preproposal strategies, customer briefing strategies, information gathering strategies, strategies for achieving customer rapport, proposal strategies, presentation strategies, and negotiation strategies. With this book, a skilled communicator can build and execute a comprehensive contract-capture plan, incorporating the strategies needed to win.

These strategies aren't presented as panaceas but are merely suggestions which have worked effectively in a majority of the instances in which they've been tried. Unlike many books on developing and implementing business strategy, this one points out that there are various roads to success. The trick is to take the route that best fits the character of your business and circumstances.

Pay particular attention to the checklists. Some of the items may seem trivial (most are just good common sense), but don't be too casual in your attitude towards them.

The basic mechanism for winning government contracts is the proposal, a written offer to provide a product or service. Critique your past proposals and you'll find at least one in which you could have done a better job simply by applying the ideas in this book.

The elements of what is presented here are common to any writing where the aim is to explain or sell. The basic advice offered throughout this book applies to new business development in all fields, although it is specifically addressed to seekers of government contracts in aerospace and related industries.

WHAT IS A PROPOSAL?

A proposal is a presentation of your solution to someone else's problem. For a complex problem, a lengthy proposal is required — often a fair-sized book — to tell your customer just how you intend to attack and solve his problem. A proposal often suggests to the customer problem areas he had not already recognized, in addition to describing a reasonable solution. Because it is directed both to engineers with detailed technical knowledge and to managers who may have considerably less detailed knowledge, the proposal must be technically accurate, concise, and well-written. A brilliant technical solution to a problem is no guarantee of a contract; if the proposal fails to show just how brilliant the technology is and how explicitly it solves the customer's problem, all the technical skill is wasted.

Proposals range all the way from letters of only a few pages to multiple volumes containing several thousand pages of text and graphics. The majority are well within these extremes, consisting of fifteen to a hundred typewritten pages. They are reproduced by some readily available means and are bound between heavy stock covers. Elaborate proposals may include a preliminary design or may even be accompanied by a video tape, or scale model of the proposed product. Most design models are made for petrochemical and nuclear energy plants, where complicated piping and safety regulations cause many engineering headaches. Design models are also used to depict buildings such as aerospace, food processing, and shipbuilding plants. But whatever the format, a proposal is an offer to do business. If it is accepted, you have a legal, binding contract.

Making the offer saleable is what proposal preparation is all about. This is done by presenting your strengths in their best light while minimizing your weaknesses (not necessarily hiding them). The danger is that your strengths and weaknesses are different on different bids, and many proposals have failed to realize this.

Companies live or die based on the success or failure of their proposals. Usually written in response to a request for proposal (RFP), a proposal presents the company's offer to sell its products and services. Proposals are competitively evaluated, and every effort should be made to produce proposals which are your ebullient best. There can be few people in management, marketing, engineering, and finance who have not been involved in proposal preparation at some time or other, for not many assignments are more vital to individuals or companies.

But for many, scientists and engineers in particular, proposal writing isn't a welcome assignment. For some it is easy to express themselves on paper; for others, it can be a trying experience. Some consider proposal writing to be in the geriatric ward of engineering assignments. The usual explanations follow.

- Some scientists and engineers, even those who are crackerjack designers, are unable to describe complicated situations in simple and clear language.
- Most engineers by nature like to design but hate to write descriptions.
- Many scientific people fear putting in writing something that may prove to be wrong.
- Widespread among engineers is the attitude that writing is drudgery.
- Some people are unable or unwilling to read their own writing objectively for possible misinterpretations. Hence, they write poorly.

Admittedly, proposal writing isn't for everyone. But for some, the work can be challenging, interesting, and gratifying.

Proposal assignments are usually short, so when the proposal effort is uninteresting or otherwise distasteful, a change in work assignment is rarely more than 30 to 45 days away. And the temporary nature of proposal assignments gives them the potential for being more exciting than other more permanent alliances. Contrast this with contract-oriented engineering assignments which can last a year or more and can sometimes be so unpleasant that they tarnish the lustre of the engineering profession.

WHAT ARE THE MAJOR ELEMENTS AND FEATURES OF A PROPOSAL?

Proposals often consist of three volumes designated technical, cost, and management proposals. Increasingly, an integrated logistics support volume is also required in government procurements. In small procurements, the management and integrated logistics support proposals are sometimes combined with the technical proposal.

The chart shown in Figure 1.1 establishes approximate guidelines for classifying proposals on the basis of the number of words used in their makeup. Four classifications, letter proposals, small proposals, medium proposals, and large proposals are included. The average number of words in sentences and paragraphs is included in the chart for reference. Note that the scale of the dependent variable (number of words) is logarithmic in order to cover the several orders of magnitude depicted.

The technical volume reveals your intended solution to the problem, showing details of your design and highlighting its important technical features and characteristics. Feasibility of meeting performance goals should be the prime discussion topic.

The management volume describes the resources that you intend to apply to the program, how you will control the work, and how you will measure work progress. It should include your proposed staffing plan for the program as well as a comprehensive schedule showing major milestones.

The integrated logistics support volume details the support that you intend to provide after delivery of the product. Reliability and maintainability engineering, which determine how long a product operates without trouble, are important ingredients of any integrated logistics support volume.

The cost volume will often resemble pages from an accountant's ledger, with minimum narrative explanation. It will also usually include

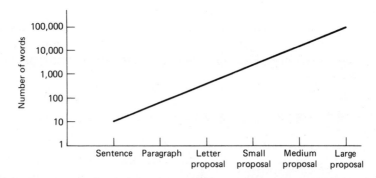

Fig. 1.1 A proposals classification system based on the number of words used in their makeup. The average number of words in sentences and paragraphs is included for reference.

the terms and conditions under which a selling price has been established, such as hour estimates, specific labor skills to be used, and expected rate of expending funds. The content of the cost volume will vary widely depending upon customer requirements for cost documentation and the type of contract anticipated. Government agencies can be very demanding in the amount of detail required in the cost volume of a proposal.

Most proposals are the assembled work of three or more people, and contrasting individualities can carry through to, and detract from, the final product unless it is skillfully edited. Sometimes, contradictory statements will slip through because not enough editing is done. Contradictions can give the customer the impression that the proposal writers don't know what they are doing. Another danger is that the proposal writers become overcautious in an effort to avoid risk, so the proposal becomes general and ambiguous "mush."

Proposed concepts sometimes little resemble the final product. An earlier (proposal stage) idealistic design is many times changed by the realities of actual development. Hindsight often reveals that a contract award was based on a proposal design which proved to be irrelevant.

A utopian goal, sought by many companies but achieved by very few is to not have to submit proposals for new business. Proposals can cost as much as $100,000 (oftentimes much more) and can consume much time. A measure of success in some businesses is when clients come to them solely on reputation and word-of-mouth endorsements, saving the costs of proposals. However, government regulations make unproposed sales impossible in many fields.

HOW IS A PROPOSAL TEAM STAFFED?

Proposal team staffing can follow any of three philosophies: (1) a dedicated proposal group that does every proposal with little or no support from others; (2) a dedicated staff of proposal specialists who are the common ingredients of every proposal but who call upon various experts for technical, management, integrated logistics support, and cost inputs; (3) no full-time proposal types, a customized "pickup" team is instead assembled for each proposal requirement. Advantages and disadvantages of these three philosophies are summarized in Figure 1.2.

PROPOSAL TEAM PHILOSOPHY	ADVANTAGE	DISADVANTAGE
1	Team can be strong and efficient in applying modern proposal techniques.	Team can quickly become technically obsolete.
2	Good balance of technical and proposal technique knowledge.	None apparent.
3	Team can have edge-of-the-art technical capabilities.	Team can be weak in basic writing skills and the application of modern proposal techniques.

Fig. 1.2 Pro's and con's for various proposal group organizations.

All proposal specialists and no proposal specialists are extremes to be avoided in the makeup of an effective proposal team. A steady diet of proposal operations can result in technical obsolescence in some individuals, causing them to resort to more and more boilerplate* in the preparation of proposals. On the other hand, total lack of experience and capabilities in the use of modern proposal techniques can result in proposals that look and sound amateurish. Therefore, a growing number of companies are recognizing the value of a more balanced approach: a few full-time proposal specialists who support recruited-as-needed technical experts.

WHO DIRECTS THE PROPOSAL EFFORT?

To write a really large proposal, say 1000 pages or more, is a formidable job which, when considered all at once, can cause some men to shrink from the immensity of the task. To write the proposal in 30 days or so requires that it be a team affair with sharing of the workload. The job should be led by a skilled proposal manager.

---

*"Boilerplate" is a proposal writer's euphemism meaning material which is used over and over with little or no modification.

For a proposal manager to be a winner, he must motivate the proposal team to respond to his leadership. He must "come across" to executive, program, and functional management as a man who knows what must be done. He must be a take-charge individual. Particularly successful proposal managers have a unique balance of technical competence, administrative ability, and human relations skills.

Oftentimes the proposal manager is assigned long before a firm bid decision is made. The proposal manager is delegated responsibility for all aspects of the proposal effort (see Figure 1.3). Technical volume, management volume, cost volume, and logistics support volume leaders are sometimes assigned to be responsible for all phases of their respective proposal volumes with overall direction from the proposal manager (see Figure 1.4). A large multivolume proposal will sometimes be coordinated by volume chairpersons who perform the technical proposal leader function for each of the various books. In smaller proposals, such as those of a research and development nature, the proposal manager might fulfill all of these functions. After selection of the manager and leaders, the proposal manager should convene a meeting to make everyone aware of the overall proposal preparation plan.

Because of the number and variety of specialists involved (writers, editors, typists, printer, etc.), the most challenging proposal management task can be to efficiently control the work flow. For example, if the typing pool runs out of work, there is the temptation to hurry or even bypass the editing in order to give the typists something to do. However, such impulsive scheduling of proposal tasks usually leads to less than satisfactory results, and oftentimes, to total rework.

HOW LONG DOES IT TAKE TO WRITE A PROPOSAL?

Typically, RFP's permit only 30 days from receipt to delivery of the completed proposal. The RFP due date establishes the end date of the proposal preparation schedule. The proposal manager sometimes prepares two schedules: (1) an ideal schedule requiring no overtime and permitting the proposal to be mailed to the customer, and (2) a "last ditch" schedule requiring evening and weekend activity and special handling for delivery. The last ditch schedule is too often the actual proposal schedule because proposal contributors have some other full-time job to perform other than proposal writing. Each engineer/author

- Coordinate preproposal activities.
- Review RFP.
- Compile BID/NO BID recommendations.
- Estimate proposal costs and obtain approved funding.
- Attend bidders conference.
- Compose summary sheet with proposal preparation schedule and distribute with RFP to key members of proposal team.
- Obtain referenced documents, e.g., specifications.
- Review technical proposal requirements (TPR) provided with the RFP.
- Compose proposal outline and establish proposal team roster. If an outline for the proposal is presented in the RFP, follow it exactly. Have all the headings of the technical specification typed out to form a detailed outline of the technical section.
- Prepare a glossary for handout to the proposal team. This will encourage common language among the various authors. Include key words and phrases that are stressed in the RFP.
- Convene kickoff meeting to discuss:
  - proposal requirements
  - outline/writing assignments/schedules
  - basic theme(s)/strategy
  - conceptual design
- Write introductory material, related experience descriptions, resumes, etc.
- Coordinate and participate in design reviews.
- Monitor and control proposal costs.
- Assemble, edit, and coordinate graphics production.
- Originate conceptual designs for cover artwork.
- Distribute total proposal preprint.
- Coordinate final editing.
- Coordinate management reviews.
- Determine and arrange for proper security and proprietary data markings.
- Comply with export and technical data disclosure regulations if proposing foreign sale of products or services.
- Proof customer copies (check for missing or improperly bound pages).
- Compose cover letter (in collaboration with Marketing).
- Arrange for proposal delivery to customer.
- Control distribution of proposal copies for internal use.
- Coordinate postproposal activities:
  - Responses to inquiries
  - Presentations
  - Demonstrations

Fig. 1.3 Checklist of Proposal Manager responsibilities. It takes a highly capable proposal professional to do all these things and do them well.

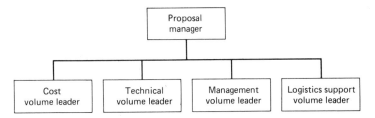

Fig. 1.4 Typical Proposal Organization. When you take on the proposal manager assignment, you are managing a special, one-shot job that has never been done before and, in all likelihood, may never be done again.

will typically have some other primary assignment, and the proposal manager sometimes must negotiate for a contributor's services from a hostile program manager.

After deciding to bid, the requirements should be reviewed in a meeting of the proposal team. When the product and/or services to be offered are defined and agreed to, the outline, schedule, and writing assignments are made.

THE PROPOSAL PREPARATION PROCESS — WHAT DOES IT LOOK LIKE?

The proposal preparation process can be viewed as a series of steps which typically proceed something like this:

- Idea
- Concept
- Outline
- Draft
- Review
- Revise
- Edit
- Draw Graphics
- Review
- Revise
- Finalize
- Final Type and Pasteup
- Print
- Deliver
- Distribute (internally)

In this process, the proposal will sometimes evolve through several draft cycles before reaching the ready-to-print, camera-ready master stage. Usually starting with some point-of-departure document, the stages of evolutionary development might look like Figure 1.5 and the number of evolutionary drafts may go as high as five, sometimes even more.

The activities and events that take place during the proposal process aren't all related to writing and editing. Figures 1.6a, 1.6b, and 1.6c outline in detail an overall proposal plan whose individual events are discussed in detail in the following chapters. The activities and events of the plan make up five phases in the preparation of the proposal.

STAGES OF PROPOSAL DEVELOPMENT	DEFINITION
Point-of-departure document	Previous proposal/study report/ IR&D report
First draft	Unedited text, 50% complete or better; some sketches in place
Second draft	All text created but not fully edited or polished; all artwork identified
.	.
.	.
.	.
Revision collection copy/ Red Team draft (see Chapters 10 and 11)	Text and artwork 100% complete
Final draft	All text complete and edited for consistency, grammar, and style; all artwork with captions in place.
Camera-ready masters	All text and artwork including cover art in place; all figures referenced, pages numbered, front matter in place.

Fig. 1.5 Stages of proposal development and their definitions.

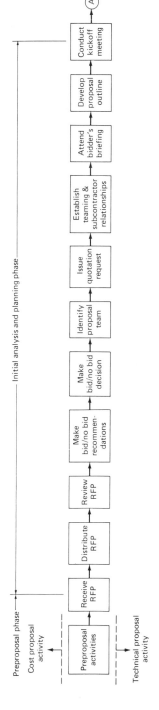

Fig. 1.6a Initial analysis and planning phase of the proposal development procedure.

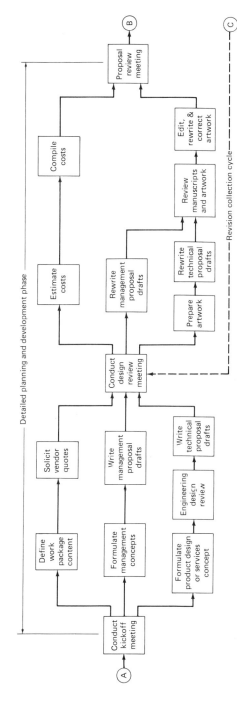

Fig. 1.6b Detailed planning and development phase of the proposal development procedure.

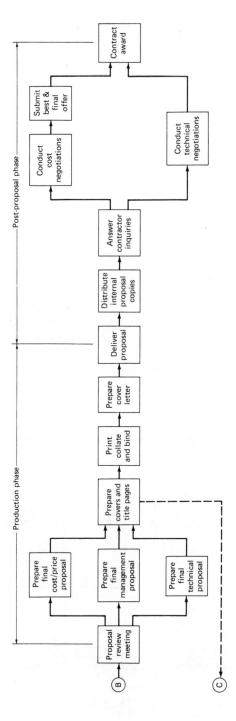

Fig. 1.6c Production and postproposal phases of the proposal development procedure.

- Preproposal Phase
- Initial Analysis and Planning Phase
- Detailed Planning and Development Phase
- Production Phase
- Postproposal Phase

As Figures 1.6a, 1.6b, and 1.6c indicate, a proposal is not completed after the first draft is written. In fact, many proposal experts maintain that when you think you've finished (that is, when you understand the problem and have explained it thoroughly in an initial draft) *then* the work begins.

Figures 1.6a, 1.6b, and 1.6c are organized with primary paths along a horizontal mid-line, above the horizontal mid-line, and below the horizontal mid-line. Milestones on the horizontal mid-line are general topics that apply to the overall proposal preparation task; above the mid-line are costing milestones, and below the mid-line are technical milestones. The number of events and the interactions among them underscore the fact that proposal preparation can be a complex, synergistic activity requiring extaordinary teamwork and cooperative spirit among its participants. Completing the entire process, doing it right, and doing it on time can be extremely satisfying — especially when it wins.

If Figures 1.6a, 1.6b, and 1.6c seem a bit overwhelming, Figure 1.7 presents a streamlined version of the same process and, in addition, provides approximate times to complete each event, assuming a typical (30-day) overall proposal schedule. The trouble with most 30-day proposals, however, is that the 30 days go by too quickly to do a decent job. You must have a significant head start before the 30-day clock begins. Hence, the preproposal effort.

Whichever plan suits your needs, make your version of it and tack it on the wall in front of your desk. Then, during actual proposal operations, cross off each event as it is completed. During large and complex efforts, this is a good way to preserve your sanity.

WHAT IS GOOD WIN/LOSS PERFORMANCE?

Your win/loss ratio isn't a highly meaningful calculation to make because one big win (or loss) can make many small ones fade into

TASK	TO BE COMPLETED BY:
Preproposal Activities	Optional
Receive and Distribute RFP	Day 1
Review RFP	Day 1
Make Bid/No Bid Decision (Consider recommendations from Marketing, Engineering, Contracts, Management, etc.)	Day 2
Estimate Proposal Budget	Day 2
Proposal Team and Assigned Proposal Manager Prepare Proposal Outline	Day 2
Convene Coordination (Kick-Off) Meeting	Day 3
Concept Formulation/Win Strategy Development	Day 3-10
Convene Coordination/Design Review Meetings	As Required
Prepare Drafts/Estimate Person-hrs. & Materials	Day 10-20
Compile First Draft/Person-Hr. Estimates/ Materials List	Day 20-23
Overall Edit	Day 23-25
Final Rewrites/Final Draft	Day 25-27
Final Type	Day 27-28
Proofread/Make Corrections	Day 28
Management Review/Cost Analysis/Price Determination	Day 28
Print	Day 29
Write Cover Letter	Day 29
Deliver to Customer	Day 30
Evaluation by Customer	As Required
Oral Presentation	As Required
Contract Award	
Postaward Debriefing	Optional

Fig. 1.7 Detailed plan and schedule for a typical (30-day) proposal.

insignificance. But for contracts which are roughly equal in size, four wins in ten submittals is a fair average; six wins in ten is a very good performance; eight in ten means you're doing virtually everything right.

It's more useful, though, to analyze your performance in greater detail. For example, what is your win/loss performance in government, commercial, and international areas? In Air Force, Navy, Army, and NASA procurements? These ratings may point up localized weaknesses for which corrective actions can be taken.

2
The Strategic Business Plan — Where It All Starts

- Why do you need a business plan?
- What should a good plan tell you?
- What are its contents?
- Who will use it?
- How often should the plan be updated?
- The causes of most business failures.

Ask a group of successful entrepreneurs what they consider to be the most important ingredient of business survival. More than a few will answer: "planning." Specifically, a long range business plan outlining objectives and tactics is recognized by experts to be the linchpin of any truly successful enterprise. Historically, many would-be entrepreneurs have been able to develop technical concepts; getting contracts has been another matter.

To those fortunate enough to have survived without giving systematic thought about where their business is coming from, a strategic business plan may be an entirely new concept, so let's look at some of its benefits.

A good business plan can tell you, for example, whether you should go after that government contract, or whether you should let it pass. A plan which defines your area of interest will show up peripheral and fringe opportunities as being of little or no help in reaching your long-range objectives.

The plan may also tell you that your chances of winning the contract are small even if you do everything right. This could be due to your competitive posture being too weak in this particular competition. A comprehensive plan, of course, will assess your competitors' strengths and weaknesses. Further, the information about markets, competitors, and relative capabilities in the business plan can help to guide future proposals, product improvements, and presentations. The savings made possible by the plan's preservation and redirection of proposal resources to the most lucrative contract opportunities can be very significant. Let's take a closer look at the ingredients of a business plan.

Figure 2.1 is an outline for a basic business plan. The plan should show that the need for the product comes from the "pull" of requirements, not from the "push" of technology. The plan should include a description of the product, pulling no punches regarding weaknesses as well as strengths. Next, the plan should define the potential market and assess the competitive situation. Finally, the plan should analyze the various costs of fully implementing the plan's recommendations.

The span of a business plan can extend six months, a year, two years, or even five years. Many businesses run five year cycles where, at the end of this time, they either expand, close, or sell out. But the more extended a plan, the greater the difficulty in fully achieving it.

All of the data in a plan make it a highly sensitive and proprietary, document. Thus, access to it should be controlled accordingly. To discourage unauthorized reading and copying, mark every page of the plan with a proprietary data legend like the one below.

PROPRIETARY INFORMATION NOTICE

This document contains information proprietary to, and is the property of, the _____ , Company. It shall not be reproduced, used or disclosed in any manner or for any purpose not authorized in writing by _____ , and except as retention may be so authoed it shall be returned to the Company upon request.

The plan is very much like an ordinary roadmap. The route isn't inflexible; alternate routes are permitted and detours can arise suddenly

1.0   Summary
2.0   Description of Product
3.0   Market Segment of Interest
4.0   Competitive Posture
5.0   Recommended Product Improvements
6.0   Cost/Price Summary

Fig. 2.1 Basic outline for a business plan. Additions such as Logistics Support Considerations may be appropriate.

and unexpectedly. But the existence of the roadmap (plan) makes selection of the best alternatives far easier than if the plan didn't exist.

A good plan will include the major areas of business and their costs as shown in Figure 2.2, laid out as milestones on a time base. This allows management and financial backers to see the complete picture before giving the go-ahead to go after that government contract. They can review the costs of implementing the plan, including milestones already accomplished and new ones which must be undertaken. And with this long-range strategic conception they can make decisions with certainty and without vacillation. The plan thus becomes a management tool for use in allocating budgets and other resources among various synergistic activities.

Earliest in the plan's sequence of events should be the establishment of a need for the product. Ideally, needs are established by customers and are identified by your marketing group.

Then, a capability or product of your company is recognized, again usually by someone in marketing, as a potential match against the forthcoming government requirement. This matchup must be specific, not just a common field of interest such as mechanical design, electronics, construction, etc.

Financial backers will normally force a more detailed planning discipline on any new undertaking than what is shown in Figure 2.2. They

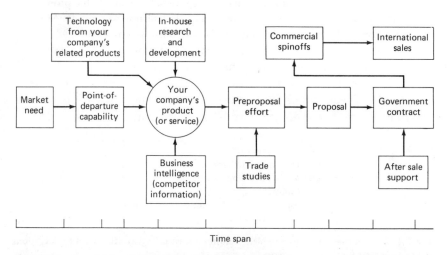

Fig. 2.2 A generalized strategic business plan for obtaining a government contract. The time span might cover 90 days, a year, five years, or some other period.

will want you to project over a multi-year period not only the major milestones of Figure 2.2, but also such things as test equipment needs, floor space requirements, number of people required, potential risks, and so on. Further strategy suggestions for the plan are listed in Figure 2.3.

The existence of a definitive business plan can also be an important builder of employee morale. People are a lot happier when they know where a company is going.

Then, as events take place you will be compelled to periodically modify the plan, keeping it current. Following the financial community's lead, ninety day intervals between updates seems about right for revising a business plan. If it's not at least that current, it may not be relevant.

Keep in mind that underestimating resource requirements and costs are the causes of most business failures. Helping you to predict these requirements and make arrangements for them is really what the business plan is all about.

BASIC BUSINESS PLAN GOALS

Without identifying a specific product or area, we cannot talk about explicit goals except the obvious one: win the contract. However, there are other implicit goals common to any product.

First, it should be a goal to be the product leader – to excel in technology, reliability, maintainability, and value. The product should be foremost in quality, being as defect-free as it can be made.

- Make use of all resources available to you. If your company has commercial, government, and international divisions, draw upon the expertise of all of them wherever it's appropriate to your plan's goals.
- Incorporate realistic and physically measurable milestones in the plan so that management and financial backers can assess progress and know when events are complete.
- Incorporate "branching" (alternative paths) if different courses of action may be warranted by actual developments. Backup plans can often be worthwhile investments.
- Show the projected rate of expending funds, person-loading forecasts versus time, and required infusions of any other kinds of support. This data should be incorporated as companion illustrations within the basic plan.
- A risk assessment should be made which delineates the potential for performance, schedule, and cost perturbations and whether their occurrence likelihood is ranked high, medium, or low.

Fig. 2.3 Strategies for preparing a strategic business plan.

Second, the quest should be to manufacture the product as efficiently as possible. Many are turning to robotics to achieve this goal.

Third, it should be a goal to compete in, and grow with, the area of the product even after the sought-after contract is completed.

RISK ASSESSMENT

Before rushing pell-mell into any business transaction, aerospace managers must look for ways to ensure lowest downside risk and highest upside potential.

Risk assessment, management, and abatement should be applied across the board both initially during the preparation of the strategic business plan and as a continuing activity during the proposal effort and then during the awarded contract. A risk assessment made as part of a strategic business plan should be thorough, aboveboard, and honest. An assessment that goes outside the company, as in a proposal, may be less candid. From a pure proposalmanship viewpoint, the objective of any risk assessment should be to show that risks have been exhaustively considered, that some risks have indeed been identified (this shows credibility) and that with proposed modern controls and measurement techniques, diligently applied, will never exceed a low or negligible risk classification. Reality, of course, often interferes with such optimism. The recommended approach to proposals is to address all risks for which satisfactory solutions can be offered and to *downplay* risks for which no satisfactory solutions can be offered.

Strategic business planners should delineate the risk assessment, analysis, and management procedures to be employed throughout the course of the plan. Techniques for identifying, monitoring, and controlling costs (including logistics support costs), and schedule risks should be identified, to include work-around solutions for anticipated problem areas and risks and the method of reporting them to the government. The organizational flow of risk management should be depicted clearly.

In the assessment include identification of the cost and schedule drivers and identify any features that might considerably increase the cost of implementing the plan without enhancing the value of the end product.

A. Identify Risks
   1. Classify and rank the risks into technical, schedule, and cost areas.
   2. Review technical, schedule, and cost requirements.
      (A) Identify areas where improvement is required.
      (B) List areas where problems yet to be solved may make it impossible to achieve required technical, schedule, or cost goals.

B. Assess the Impact of Identified Risks
   1. Technical Impact – Will performance be degraded? How much?
   2. Schedule Impact – Will additional time be required to develop solution? Are there any alternatives? How long will each take?
   3. Cost Impact – Will additional funds be required to solve the problem? How much?

C. Formulate Risk Reduction Actions
   1. What can be done to reduce risk? To avoid risk altogether?
   2. What alternative approaches are there?

Fig. 2.4 Generalized risk assessment and management procedure.

When the RFP comes out, identify any moderate and high risk areas which are forced upon you by the specific requirements of the RFP. The government is extremely interested in any areas of their system specifications involving high technical risk. Each offeror is encouraged to identify these areas and propose alternative technical solutions.

Risks should also be classified as to their impact on cost, schedule, and performance, and they should be quantified as to severity (high, moderate, low, or negligible). A generalized procedure is summarized in Figure 2.4. A sample risk analysis for a hypothetical program is presented in Figure 2.5. Areas are designated as having performance, cost, or schedule influence and are classified as having high, moderate, or low risk.

POTENTIAL RISK	TYPE OF RISK (COST, SCHEDULE, OR PERFORMANCE)	RISK CLASSIFICATION (HIGH, LOW, OR MODERATE)	RISK ABATEMENT PLAN
a. Long Lead Item Procurements – Not Enough Time	S	M	a. Prepare for long item procurements on an approved pre-award basis.
b. Incomplete Prototype/Brassboard Testing – Not Enough Time	S,C,P	L	b. Multiple shift testing.
c. Computer Run-Time Specifcation – Too Demanding	C	M	c. Reprogram for improved run-time.
d. Design Data Availability	S,C	L	d. Use alternative data based on assumptions, estimations, extrapolations, interpolations, judgment, and experience.

Definitions

High   — Success very much in doubt — requires extreme effort and management attention/planning.
Moderate — Success will require considerable management attention/planning.
Low   — Success assured with come management attention.

Fig. 2.5 A sample Risk Assessment Summary and Risk Abatement Plan. Risks are classified as to their impact on cost, schedule, or performance and qualified as to severity.

3
Business Intelligence — Getting Competitor/Customer Information and Using It

- Intelligence sources, what are they?
- Aboveboard, a bit shady, and strictly underhanded methods.
- How to use the information after you get it.
- Reverse engineering, is it worth the cost?

Most companies can't rely entirely on their innate technical superiority to win contracts. A "we're doing alright, head in sand" attitude can lead to rude awakenings. This is especially true in the fast-moving aerospace and electronics industries. Companies in these fields must engage in continuous and purposeful business intelligence activities to avoid being suddenly scuttled by someone else's revolutionary developments.

Despite the covert implications of the word "intelligence," these activities aren't necessarily unlawful or even mysterious or secretive. Most are simply intelligent and necessary business practices.

When companies are caught by surprise, it can sometimes be attributed to a breakdown in business intelligence or a failure to react to intelligence inputs. Unprecedented demand for small, fuel-efficient cars instead of gas guzzlers, a precipitous drop in demand for electromechanical desk calculators, and the sudden emergence of incredible computer-aided manufacturing tools and processes for the production of electronic circuit boards are examples which come to mind. A low-cost typewriter that can take dictation could devastate and transform large segments of the typewriter, word processing, and computer industries if it emerged suddenly without warning. Business intelligence could soften the blow by allowing savvy competitors to react sooner.

The main business intelligence task is to gather and interpret information. Here, company marketeers are usually the most fruitful source of information about upcoming procurements and about the activities of competitors. Other valuable sources are technical journals and magazines, professional society meetings, and seminars. Professional meetings sponsored or co-sponsored by a military or government agency can be particularly valuable since a "requirements" paper or an advanced planning briefing will many times be presented. These briefings often include current information on plans, policies, and programs in support of future requirements.

But what about the other less accepted ways of gathering information? Figure 3.1 lists some of these in contrast to a few of the "acceptable" activities.

Your marketeers, or someone charged with the responsibility for business intelligence data gathering, should be able to come up with publications and other worthwhile information regarding any forthcoming procurement.

Straight Arrow
- Gleaning information from briefings, trade journals, news releases, stockholder reports, professional societies, and published study reports
- Hiring key competitor personnel for their abilities
- Forthrightly ask a competitor
- Forthrightly ask a customer
- Data requests in accordance with the Freedom of Information Act

A Tad Less Than Sportsmanlike
- Receipt of material not given to all
- Hiring key competitor personnel for the information that they have
- Pressuring vendors and subcontractors for information about competitors, e.g., what computer capacity is asked for in the competitor's quotation request?
- Disseminating false intelligence to mislead competitors

Foul Play
- Infiltration (Spy in competitor's organization)
- Obtaining competitor briefing handouts; ignoring their proprietary restrictions and markings
- Covert photography
- Information leaks from print shops
- Bribes
- Pilfering
- Electronic surveillance

Fig. 3.1 Information gathering strategies.

A CASE HISTORY

Bidders can sometimes learn a great deal from the published works of known evaluators. Once, an evaluator on a large computer-oriented procurement had published several articles on computer selection methods. His articles were carefully analyzed and the computer selection in at least one proposal was modified to be in harmonious agreement with the evaluator's views on the subject.

DAY-TO-DAY INTELLIGENCE SOURCES

Business intelligence comes to us from many sources, including newspapers, newsletters, trade magazines, trade shows, scientific journals, seminars, proceedings, textbooks, etc. Of contemporary note are the data search firms whose researchers prepare in-depth reports on scientific subfields for sale to special interest organizations.

Intelligence from the usual, most popular sources can be like getting a speedier tennis ball — it benefits both sides giving advantage to neither. The really valuable material comes from sources not available to everyone. Private communications, obscure published works, foreign translations, and unique personal experiences can provide these kinds of competitive edges.

When you get an intelligence-derived edge, protect it. Patent it if you can. Don't reveal it prematurely in a publication. Don't let anyone and everyone have access to it — especially employees likely to leave for greener pastures. Even revealing the reason for your technical superiority in a proposal may prove to be unwise, as the section in this book dealing with the Freedom of Information Act will show.

BUYING BUSINESS INTELLIGENCE FROM A MARKET RESEARCH FIRM

For an annual fee, a subscriber can get a report plus regular updates on a particular industry. The information is gathered, packaged in an organized way, and sold by professional market research firms. Time is an important element of the process since the information must be disseminated soon enough to aid decision making. At least fifteen companies gather, process, and sell this kind of business intelligence as their primary activity.

The information is sold in several ways. Custom research in which the information is provided to a single client is the most expensive. This is followed by multi-client market reports in which several users share the cost of the research. Least expensive are the newsletters and periodicals which are made available to many subscribers. Both the quality and price of market research products can vary widely. The leaders in market research are listed below.

Arthur D. Little, Cambridge, MA
Auerbach Associates, Philadelphia, PA
Booz, Allen & Hamilton, New York, NY
Chilton Research Services, Radnor, PA
Creative Strategies International, San Jose, CA
Datapro Research, Delran, NJ
Dataquest, Menlo Park, CA
Diebold Group, New York, NY
Gnostic Concepts, Menlo Park, CA
Input, Menlo Park, CA
International Data, Newtonville, MA
Predicasts, Cleveland, OH
Quantum Science, New York, NY
SRI International, Menlo Park, CA
Strategic Business Services, San Jose, CA

FREEDOM OF INFORMATION ACT REQUESTS

The Freedom of Information Act (FOIA), passed in 1967, provides anyone the right to request and, in most cases, receive documents from the U.S. government. Even competitor proposals, prepared at great expense, can be obtained by anyone making a FOIA request for them. The agency providing the requested documents need only charge fees to cover the costs of search and duplication.

If an agency declines your FOIA request, appeal and litigation steps can be taken that can overcome capricious withholding of information by agency personnel. This, of course, carries the attendant risk of alienating a customer.

Identified in the FOIA are nine categories of documents that the government may rightfully withhold. A brief summarization of these exceptions follows.

1. Classified information.
2. Certain government internal rules and policies.
3. Documents containing trade secrets or financial information which a government component receives on a privileged or confidential basis.
4. Information excluded by law from public release.
5. Internal communications among government agencies.
6. Certain personal information about an individual.
7. Investigatory information.
8. Matters related to the regulation of financial institutions.
9. Geological and geophysical information concerning wells.

Item No. 3 is the only exemption likely to be invoked to prevent disclosure of unclassified technical proposals to requestors.

Contractors can discourage, but not necessarily prevent FOIA disclosure of technical proposal data by marking the title page with the following legend.

THIS DATA, FURNISHED IN CONNECTION WITH REQUEST FOR PROPOSAL NO. _____ SHALL NOT BE DISCLOSED OUTSIDE THE GOVERNMENT AND SHALL NOT BE DUPLICATED, USED, OR DISCLOSED IN WHOLE OR IN PART FOR ANY PURPOSE OTHER THAN TO EVALUATE THE PROPOSAL —PROVIDED, THAT IF A CONTRACT IS AWARDED TO THIS OFFEROR AS A RESULT OF OR IN CONNECTION WITH THE SUBMISSION OF THIS DATA, THE GOVERNMENT SHALL HAVE THE RIGHT TO DUPLICATE, USE, OR DISCLOSE THE DATA TO THE EXTENT PROVIDED IN THE CONTRACT. THIS RESTRICTION DOES NOT LIMIT THE GOVERNMENT'S RIGHT TO USE INFORMATION CONTAINED IN THE DATA IF IT IS OBTAINED FROM ANOTHER SOURCE WITHOUT RESTRICTION. THE DATA SUBJECT TO THIS RESTRICTION IS CONTAINED IN SHEETS _____

Whether or not this title page legend is honored is a matter addressed by the government on a case-by-case basis. It can be far more effective, of course, than no legend at all.

Special care should also be taken to mark sensitive proposal pages as proprietary in order to protect them from unwanted disclosure. You should mark each page that you wish to restrict with the following legend.

> "FURNISHED IN CONFIDENCE AND SUBJECT
> TO EXEMPTION UNDER 5 USC 552(B)"

In reality though, when a contractor submits a proposal to the government, he has little control over its disclosure to others. Contractors seem to be generally unaware of the ease with which they can obtain competitor proposals on completed procurements through application of the FOIA provisions. Likewise, they seem to be equally unaware of the ease with which their own proposal secrets can be compromised.

To request documents under the Freedom of Information Act, cite Public Law 93-502, as amended November 21, 1974. Indicate in your request that search and duplication costs will be accepted, or that you will accept costs up to a specified limit. Although exact nomenclature isn't required, be as specific as possible in identifying the documents of interest.

REVERSE ENGINEERING

Reverse engineering is a sophisticated form of comparison shopping in which companies obtain and take apart their competitors' products to find out how they work. Although there has long been a popular association between reverse engineering and industrial espionage, the link isn't necessarily automatic. Reverse engineering itself isn't illegal; the use of information obtained by reverse engineering might be. However, it isn't illegal to copy a product that isn't protected by patent, trademark, or copyright.

Reverse engineering is widespread in the semiconductor, appliance, auto, camera, computer, and home entertainment industries.

What can you learn from reverse engineering? For starters, you can learn who your competitors' suppliers are from brand logos and other part markings. For another, you can make up competitors' parts lists and estimate manufacturing costs from them. And, by making performance measurements (frequency response, power consumption, speed, horsepower, etc.) you can rate your own product's comparative performance. You can thereby learn how to focus your advertising so that it exploits competitors' weaknesses and underscores your relative strengths.

But among the things that reverse engineering won't tell you are the manufacturers' production methods and, in some cases, the artistic talent needed to manufacture the product. These can be vital ingredients.

4
The All-Important Preproposal Effort

- The preproposal effort — why you must have one.
- What kind of activities make up a typical preproposal effort?
- Some tried and tested early strategies.
- How to influence the RFP.
- How to get RFP's.
- How to analyze RFP's.
- How much should the winning proposal cost?
- How to decline to bid.

Experienced proposal writers know the feeling that it sometimes doesn't seem to matter what is said in the proposal, the outcome of the proposal competition appears preordained. Often, this feeling is caused by other competitors who have done a better job on their homework. When they've wisely invested in a purposeful preproposal effort and, for one reason or another, you haven't and are going into the competition cold, that feeling of futility is probably justified. If you, as a prospective bidder, haven't influenced the *content* of the RFP, you might as well not bid at all.

What does a company do in a preproposal effort? When the forthcoming proposal is to be similar to a proposal written in the past, the preproposal task can be clear-cut. Draft copies of that earlier effort should be distributed to members of the preproposal team with instructions to revise and annotate it based upon what is known about the upcoming requirement. The team should consider possible revisions of earlier strategy as well as improved system concepts and tradeoffs that may differ from the previous effort.

You should maintain a working file of actual proposal material (technical sections, cover letters, graphics, etc.) that brought favorable response from reviewers and evaluators earlier. By modifying specifics, these can be used over and over, especially for similar proposals to different agencies.

A vital preproposal task is to get to know the customer. The forthcoming RFP may prove to be ambiguous — what does he really want? The customer may not realize the full implications of what he wants to do. The proposal must be addressed to the exact problem the customer has in mind. If he wants a widget that costs $100,000 and you propose a million-dollar, time-shared, super-widget complex, he may not even ask you to bid on his next problem, unless you can show him that the small widget will not do the job he has in mind. At the same time, you need to know who in the customer's firm is going to read the proposal so that you can address it to the proper audience with the proper technical level, getting the proper message across to the proper people.

Your marketeers should maintain a customer relations program that continues year-around, not one that's active only during the preproposal, proposal, and postproposal periods. Plant tours, new product demonstrations, special briefings, access to prestige information (e.g., preprints) are just a few of the ways that can keep customer contacts alive and favorable. Having one of your scientists or engineers coauthor a journal paper or symposium presentation with your customer is another way to cement a good relationship.

There are other tasks that can be accomplished before the formal RFP arrives. Some recommended ones are listed in Figure 4.1.

BRIEFINGS

A well-known marketing view is that the key to winning contracts is to get your most talented technical people into the customer's agency to make presentations, ask and answer questions, and generally become known to the evaluators *before the RFP is released.* There are obvious advantages in becoming well known and making a favorable impression. Most competitors, of course, also know about the value of personal contacts and will also try their utmost to get more than equal time in the customer's shop.

A customer briefing is one of the most effective personal contact activities that you can undertake. They're sometimes difficult to arrange

- Make a preliminary system design.

- Update key personnel resumes.

- Collect and review related previous proposals.

- Plan and initiate a capture strategy.

- Initiate a technical "get smart" plan:
  - do library research.
  - get related government research reports.

- Conduct customer discussions and briefings:
  - find out what he really wants.
  - tell him how to do it (in very broad terms).
  - convince him you're best qualified.

- Make your own model of the RFP.

- Do experimental outlining that highlights pet ideas.

- Start preparing proposal material, e.g., a "strawman" or artificial proposal in response to the model RFP.

- Formulate themes.

- Size up the competition:
  - list their strengths.
  - list their weaknesses.

- Count your blessings – that is, assess your own strengths:
  - facilities.
  - personnel.
  - background.
  - techniques.

- Develop teaming and subcontracting relationships.

- Develop and/or expand resources: engineering, manufacturing, test, etc.

- Get vendor specifications and quotes.

- Get copies of applicable military standards and specifications.

- Help the customer develop the RFP by assisting his technical analysis and preparation of specification.

- Hire a distinguished scientist, engineer, academician, or administrator who has specialized knowledge of the forthcoming procurement.

- Conduct trade-off studies to allocate system functions between hardware and software.

Fig. 4.1 Preproposal strategies.

- Try to get evaluators and evaluation influencers in the audience.
- Use key people.
- Make a trial presentation of your "strawman" proposal in summary form.
- Expose only the main ideas.
- Establish rapport.
- Get reflective response. Encourage customer to discuss with you his technical concerns.
- Determine your company's image as a contractor and what can be done to improve that image.
- To force the issue in an "unsolicited" situation, conclude by asking, "May we submit a written proposal?"

Fig. 4.2 Customer briefing strategies.

because of the equal consideration doctrine under which government evaluators must operate. Usually, customer briefings are set up by marketeers and take place either at your facility or at the customer's. Figure 4.2 gives a few strategy suggestions.

The format of a briefing will depend on circumstances, but a generalized sequence of topics suitable as a starting point for most customer briefings is given in Figure 4.3.

As soon as you can after the briefing, jot down your reactions along with any key points that came up during discussions. Also, note the customer reactions, if any. These notes will serve to guide your proposal themes and strategy. For example, you may want to reinforce a good point or buttress a weak argument *after* a briefing. Send a follow-up thank you letter, hitting the point you want to make. It's also a good way to get your company's name in front of him . . . again.

A bidders' briefing may or may not be conducted by the procuring agency to present clarifying details about the forthcoming procurement. The RFP may be issued before or during this briefing. The

- Introduction and Summary:
  - objectives
  - background
  - related efforts
- Operational considerations.
- Design oriented issues.
- Conclusions.

Fig. 4.3 Format of a customer briefing.

technical and contractual personnel of the procuring activity normally explain what they mean in the specifications and other items of the bid set. A "bid set" includes all of the documents that make up the RFP, including technical and cost matters, as well as briefing notes resulting from the briefing session.

They may also notify you of changes in the product or services wanted, changes in the deadline for the proposals, and other details. Company representatives attending these briefings may ask technical and contractual questions to aid the preparation of their proposals. One problem in bidders' briefings is that competitors may gain valuable information from the type of questions you ask.

GOVERNMENT PROCUREMENT TECHNIQUES

The government uses a number of different techniques to procure supplies and services. The method used is largely a function of the developmental status of the sought-after commodity, that is, whether or not it has ever been produced before and whether it is available from more than one source. The following sections briefly summarize the various procurement techniques and indicate how each one is used.

Invitations For Bids

This is an advertised procurement in which contract award is based upon the lowest offered price. The proposal must offer performance and delivery at least equal to the minimum standards established by the IFB. An IFB is usually a sealed bid situation in which there is only one opportunity to offer the winning price. A detailed technical proposal may or may not be required, but offerors will normally have to prequalify as established suppliers of the commodity to be procured.

Sole-Source Procurements

If your company is in the enviable position of being the sole manufacturer of a particular commodity, the government may sometimes enter into a sole-source arrangement with you. Also sole-source procurements have been made in time of war when a quick reaction has been needed to counter a sudden or potential enemy threat. Most often, this has occurred in the field of electronic warfare. However, because of its weak bargaining position, the government discourages the use of sole-source arrangements whenever another procurement method can be applied.

Negotiated Procurements

The most common method of procurement is the negotiated procurement in which a procuring contracting officer conducts negotiations with the offerors who have been determined to be responsive and competitive. A negotiated procurement is usually implemented by an RFP, which is distributed to offerors who respond to public advertisements.

Two-Step Advertised Procurements

A two-step procurement is one in which the government first solicits unpriced proposals and later asks for cost proposals from the offerors who submitted acceptable proposals in Step 1. The Step 1 solicitation might include technical, management, and integrated logistics support components.

Four-Step Advertised Procurements

In this method of procurement, the contractor submits an unpriced technical proposal during Step 1. That is, he submits all required submittals with the exception of the cost volume. The government's goal at this stage is to gain an appreciation and understanding of the proposal by identifying areas requiring amplification or clarification. A listing of these areas needing clarification is prepared for each contractor.

Discussions are then held with each offeror, usually preceded by the offeror "walking" the government through his proposal. The ensuing discussions are for the purpose of requesting amplification or clarification. Offerors are not advised of deficiencies in their proposals. Ideally, the areas needing amplification or clarification will have been provided to each offeror in advance of the discussions. No conclusions regarding the merits of the proposal are made at this time.

In Step 2, the offeror submits amplifications and/or clarifications to his proposal (as he deems appropriate), together with a cost proposal.

A competitive price range determination is made by the government. It is unlikely that any firm will be eliminated at this point, but it is possible. There is no provision in this step (or in Step 1) for rejection on the basis of technical or cost unacceptability, only for being beyond the competitive price range.

A second round of discussions is now held, focusing upon cost. Technical factors may again be discussed, as necessary, subject to the non-divulgence of the deficiencies rule of Step 1, which includes the requirement for review prior to discussions of those areas requiring additional amplification or clarification. At the conclusion of the second round of discussions, a second competitive price range determination is made. At the conclusion of this step, a final proposal (best and final offer) is requested.

In Step 3, the offeror's final technical and cost proposals are received. A single source is then selected for preliminary negotiation of a definitive contract. (Note he is *not* selected for award.) Particular care will be exercised by the government not to reveal competitive approaches, features, and costs during this preliminary negotiation because in Step 4 the cost and technical aspects may be negotiated with *any* of the offerors. Accordingly, although an offeror may not be an apparent winner for preliminary negotiations due to "scoring," he may well become the selected source for negotiations should his proposal offer the greatest potential to become the best value.

In Step 4, an in-depth final negotiation is held. Should agreement not be reached in the time set by the contracting officer, the government may extend the time or cease negotiations. The procurement may be pursued with the second choice offeror, or cancelled. Contract award concludes the four-step procedure.

"Fly-Off" Competitions

Some contracts involve more than one stage, the first stage being used to reduce many proposals to the two or three best possibilities, and then a final stage being used to choose the best approach for production. After building the prototypes, an evaluation is made of both the prototype and a production proposal submitted by each offeror. The production contract award is made on the basis of both performance of the prototypes and evaluation of the written proposals.

HOW TO GET RFP'S

The principal vehicle by which RFP's are obtained is the response to formal solicitation announcements in the *Commerce Business Daily,* a U.S. Department of Commerce publication. The CBD, as it is called, is a daily list of U.S. Government procurement invitations, contract awards, subcontracting leads, sales of surplus property, and foreign business opportunities. A model framework for responding to a CBD announcement of a forthcoming research and development solicitation is shown in Figure 4.4.

You should prepare a "boilerplate" write-up for use as a standard attachment to all such capabilities letters. The write-up should include the following information.

- Brief summary of company activities.
- Description of company facilities plus affiliates in terms of usage (engineering, manufacturing, administration, etc), floor space and people
- Total number of scientists and engineers.
- Statement summarizing security clearance status of facilities and people.
- Statement certifying whether company is classified as small business. (Companies having fewer than 500, 750, 1000, or 1500 employees are classified by the U.S. Government as "small businesses." The RFP will provide the applicable size standard.)

HOW TO ANALYZE RFP'S

An RFP will often include all of the sections listed in Figure 4.5. Figure 4.5 classifies the various RFP sections according to their importance to the customer and to the bidders. Within the labyrinthine makeup of the RFP, the first three of the sections listed are of primary significance to the proposal writer.

1. Statement of Work (SOW)
2. Specification
3. Proposal Preparation Instructions

The SOW and specification will usually determine, more than anything else, whether your company should bid or not bid for the contract.

COMPANY LETTERHEAD

XXXXXXXX X, XXXX

XXXXXX XXXXXX XXXXXX XXXXXX XXXXXX
XXXXXXXXX, XXXX   XXXX

Attention: Code XXXXXX

Subject: Synopsis No. XXX
            XXXXX XXXXX XXXXXXXXXXXXXXXXX

Reference: Commerce Business Daily, Issue No. PSA-XXXXX
            Dated XXXX XX, XXXX

Gentlemen:

This letter is submitted by the XXXXX Company in response
to the subject requirement as outlined in the Commerce
Business Daily, Issue No. PSA-XXX, dated XXXX XX, XXXX. The
capabilities described in this letter and enclosures relate
to our experience in the area of XXXXXXX XXXXXXX XXXXXXXXXXX.

RELATED EXPERIENCE
XXXXXXXXXXXXXXXXXX

PERSONNEL

The resumes of our personnel experienced in XXXXXX XXXXXXXXX
XXXXXXXXXXXXXXX design and development are included as attachments to this letter.

FACILITIES

Facilities information and industrial security clearance data
are attached.

SUMMARY

Our experience in the development of XXXXXXX XXXXXXX XXXXXXXXX
is directly applicable to the requirement as outlined in the
Commerce Business Daily announcement. We are currently involved
in similar work. We would welcome an opportunity to demonstrate
both our capabilities and interest in the subject program through
submittal of a formal proposal.

                         Very truly yours,

                         THE XXXXXXX COMPANY

                         XXXXXXXX X. XXXXXXX, Director
                         New Business Development
XXX:sm
Attachments: Facilities Description
              Security Clearance Data, Resumes

Fig. 4.4 Example letter request for an RFP.

RFP SECTION	SIGNIFICANCE TO CUSTOMER	SIGNIFICANCE TO BIDDERS
Statement of Work	Work to be Performed	Work to be Performed
System Specification	Required System Performance	Basis for Acceptance Test
Proposal Preparation Instructions	Establishes a Common Basis for Comparing Proposals	Determines Proposal Content and Level of Detail
Work Breakdown Structure	Basis for Price Breakdown	Basis for Tasks and Cost Estimates
Contract Line Items	Required Deliverables and Basis for Payment	Required Deliverables and Basis for Payment
Contract Data Requirements List	Required Data Items and Basis for Payment	Required Data Items and Basis for Payment
Program Schedule	Milestones and Delivery Dates	Basis for Program Planning and Allocation of Resources
Cost Proposal Ground Rules	Basis for Negotiated Price	Basis for Estimating Costs
Terms and Conditions	Contractual Ground Rules	Basis for Future Changes

Fig. 4.5 Analyzing the RFP from the customer's viewpoint and from the bidder's viewpoint.

In essence, they determine what is to be done in the performance of the job.

The proposal preparation instructions will state what needs to be included in the proposal. These instructions may also specify the format requirements, evaluation factors, page limits, level of detail desired, and so on.

Next in importance is the specification, which establishes the performance and construction standards to be met. Procurements of an R&D nature will often not include a specification; instead, broad performance parameters are integrated into the SOW. This is necessary because in research and development, there are often no specifications adequate to describe an item being procured.

There is, in fact, a trend away from detailed specifications in the U.S. Government procurements. Instead, contractors are encouraged to propose their own technical approach, design features, and alternatives to cost, schedule, and capability. The philosophy is to meet broad

functional requirements rather than detailed performance requirements. This indeed seems to make a great deal of sense and should be
a healthy stimulant to competition.

Finally, the proposal preparation instructions dictate what the proposal must contain. The instructions always should be followed *TO
THE LETTER* because they constitute the checklist used by evaluators
to score your proposal.

In analyzing these three sections and related parts of the RFP, the
reviewer should look for the items in Figure 4.6. These will have the
greatest influence on your bid/no bid decision.

Shall Versus Will

In some RFP's the words "shall" and "will" have distinctly separate
meanings. "Shall" is used to express binding requirements; "will" is

- What is the required delivery date for the proposal?
- What is the required delivery time for the product or services to be procured?
- Is the requirement a small business set-aside? (That is, is the procurement restricted only
  to bidders qualifying as small businesses?)
- Is there a "hardware exclusion clause?" (That is, is the successful bidder excluded from bid-
  ding on the later hardware procurement phases of the program. This is sometimes done
  to prevent bias of study results toward self interests.)
- Are special tools, tooling, test equipment, or facilities needed? Does it require specially
  airconditioned, dust-free, RF noise-free clean rooms, or other special environmental con-
  ditions?
- Will Government Furnished Equipment (GFE) be used?
- What are the documentation requirements?
- What are the criteria for acceptance?
- What are the reliability and maintainability (R/M) requirements? Is environmental testing
  required?
- What type of contract is contemplated?
- What is the recommended level of effort or dollar magnitude?
- What are the security clearance requirements for personnel? For the facility?
- Will the contract be a continuation of earlier work? Whose? Is it documented?
- Are there any special requirements; e.g., a benchmark demonstration?
- Who is available to write the proposal? Who can perform the job when it's awarded?
- Is a performance bond a prerequisite of any contract award?
- What are the proposal evaluation criteria?
- Are there any surprises? If so, why? Has the competition influenced the RFP?

Fig. 4.6 Checklist for analyzing RFP's.

used for nonmandatory directions or suggestions. However, this isn't a universal interpretation. Sometimes "shall" is used to specify all requirements and suggestions whereas "will" is used to express or confirm the contractor's intent to comply. In situations where precise definition of "shall" versus "will" is critical, ask for clarification.

Marketing Review Of The RFP

A member of the marketing team should review the RFP, the competition, the customer's evaluation techniques, and the relative standing of the company with the customer; estimate the price needed to win; estimate the competition's probable price; and determine any other data affecting the bid strategy.

Alternate Proposals

Occasionally, offerors may submit two proposals on the same procurement. One will be a basic proposal fully compliant with the stated requirements. The other will be a less expensive proposal usually with certain stated exceptions to the specifications. Alternate proposals however are rarely successful in competitive procurements. The reason seems to be that no approved standard can exist to compare the merits of the alternate, thus necessitating difficult judgments on the part of the evaluators. An alternate proposal is seldom prepared to the same level of detail as the basic, and its very existence can detract from an offeror's apparent confidence in his basic submittal. In short, alternate proposals are dubious investments.

UNSOLICITED PROPOSALS

In an unsolicited proposal, the contractor initiates a sole source offer without first receiving a proposal request. The strategy is to obtain outside financing for a supposed good idea or to announce and establish a position of leadership in an emerging technology. Usually written in pursuit of smaller research and development contracts, the unsolicited proposal gives much latitude in standards of format, order of presentation, content, and style. Most agencies insist that the unsolicited proposal meet basic requirements in these areas, but resourceful proposal writers find much more room for being creative than they do in the highly structured solicited procurements.

Keep in mind that unsolicited proposals can be very long-shot propositions; government budgets are already tightly apportioned among planned-for programs leaving few resources for sponsoring the unexpected. A good idea, however, will get its deserved attention, especially if an economic saving can be shown relative to the status quo.

The sequence of events in a successful unsolicited proposal are as follows.

1. Get the attention of the customer.
2. Convert attention into interest in the idea or product.
3. Convert interest into conviction.
4. Following conviction, create desire.
5. Obtain commitment.

To illustrate an unsolicited proposal, let's assume that your company has discovered a material and process for storage and retrieval. The process, known as thermography, has the potential for competing favorably with alternative methods. Verbal discussions with a military agency have shown that storage and retrieval of personnel records is a potential application. Your company decides to submit an unsolicited proposal, hoping to obtain funding for continued development. Figure 4.7 shows the outline for the technical/management volume. A separate cost volume, not shown, is assumed.

The government does not have to buy your unsolicited offering, of course, and cases have been known in which ideas in an earlier unsolicited proposal were used as the basis for a later competitive solicitation. The originator's sole source advantage was thereby lost.

HOW MUCH SHOULD THE WINNING PROPOSAL COST?

In most companies, the extent and staffing of the proposal effort is likely to be based on emotion, whim, or time available. It should be based on more sound business considerations. The amount of money spent should be established by a realistic assessment of the company's chance to win and the amount of return expected in the event of contract award. Stated mathematically, the following equation includes these factors and provides a basis for establishing the proposal budget.

1.0 SUMMARY AND INTRODUCTION
    1.1   Explanation of unsolicited basis of proposal
    1.2   Purpose of proposal
    1.3   Organization of proposal
    1.4   Statement of expected results

2.0 IDEAL CHARACTERISTICS OF A MATERIAL FOR REUSABLE
    GRAPHIC STORAGE
    2.1   Resolution – the material should ideally be grainless
    2.2   Image Retention – the desired objective is to achieve controlled image permanence
    2.3   Reusability – infinite reusability is preferred but a limited number of reuse cycles
        is acceptable
    2.4   Thickness – the material should be as thin as possible consistent with practical
        limitations of mechanical handling devices
    2.5   Electrostatic Charge – should be controllable so as not to cause image degradation
        or handling problems
    2.6   Contrast – continuous tone capability preferred but eight or more discrete gray
        shades are acceptable
    2.7   Exposure Latitude – typical ambient conditions should not cause irreversible
        changes in the material

3.0 CANDIDATE MATERIALS AND PROCESSES FOR STORAGE AND
    RETRIEVAL OR GRAPHIC INFORMATION
    3.1   Photochromism/Phototropism – optical exposure with slow, automatic recovery
    3.2   Tenebrescence – optical exposure with recovery caused by heat or exposure to dif-
        ferent wavelengths
    3.3   Electrostatic/Xerographic Recording – optical exposure with toner development
        and solvent erasure
    3.4   Surface Deformation Photoplastic and Thermoplastic Recording – electrostatic or
        magnetic field imaging with thermal erasure
    3.5   Magneto-Optical (Manganese-Bismuth) – optical exposure in the presence of a mag-
        netic field with thermal erasure
    3.6   Liquid Crystals – color change in response to heat or electric field
    3.7   Thermographic Recording – optical exposure in the presence of a magnetic field
        with erasure by exposure to high temperature

4.0 DETAILED DESCRIPTION OF THE PREFERRED TECHNIQUE
    4.1   Properties of Thermographic Material
    4.2   How Information is Stored
    4.3   How Information Is Viewed
    4.4   How Information Is Duplicated
    4.5   How Information Is Erased

5.0 EXPERIMENTAL VERIFICATION OF THE PREFERRED TECHNIQUE
    5.1   Refinement of material characteristics to enhance image quality
    5.2   Image recording using a computer – controlled laser scanner

Fig. 4.7 Proposal for investigating a reusable graphic storage medium.

6.0 PROGRAM PLAN
    6.1 Tasks to be Performed
    6.2 Manloading, Travel, and Material
    6.3 Subcontract Manloading, Travel, and Material
    6.4 Demonstration of Results

7.0 STAFFING PLAN
    7.1 Personnel Resumes Including Principal Investigator
    7.2 Subcontract Personnel

8.0 RELATED EXPERIENCE
    8.1 Human Readable/Machine Readable Information Processor
    8.2 Video Film Converter
    8.3 Automated Microfilm Aperture Card Updating System
    8.4 Tactical Image Interpretation Facility

9.0 FACILITIES AND EQUIPMENT DATA
    9.1 Description of Company Research Facilities
    9.2 Description of Available Instrumentation

Fig. 4.7 Proposal for investigating a reusable graphic storage medium (continued).

$$\text{Recommended Proposal Budget} = \frac{\rho \times \text{Contract Value}}{25}$$

Where,

ρ = the estimated probability of contract award to you, and

$1/25$ = a factor empirically determined by available funds, sales objectives, and how important the program is to the welfare of your company.

By this equation we say that a worthwhile expenditure on a given proposal is determined by the expected dollar value of the contract, the estimated probability of success, and an assortment of other considerations which contribute to the makeup of the empirical factor.

The probability of contract award to you (ρ) is the product of two other probabilities, the probability of winning and the probability of funding. The probability of winning can be intuitively selected from the following table of empirical ranges.

0.7 and above = Excellent Chance
0.5 to 0.6   = Good Chance
0.3 to 0.4   = Fair Chance
Below 0.3   = Poor Chance

**Table 4.1 Coming to Terms with Proposal Costs:
Some Representative Proposal Budgets**

CONTRACT VALUE	RECOMMENDED PROPOSAL BUDGET	
	$\rho = 0.3$	$\rho = 0.05$
$ 500,000	$ 6,000	$ 1,000
1M	12,000	2,000
5M	60,000	10,000
10M	120,000	20,000
100M	1.2M	0.2M
500M	6M	1M

The probability of funding is limited to 0.5 or below simply because of the 50/50 likelihood of program cancellation (no award) that happens so often in government procurements.

The probability of award to you then is,

$$\text{Probability of Award } (\rho) = \text{Probability of Winning} \times \text{Probability of Funding}$$

Let's assume that ρ is calculated to be 0.3 for a series of different contract values. Then we'll assume that ρ is calculated to be much lower, say 0.05, for the same series of contract values. What is the recommended proposal budget for each case? Table 4.1 gives the results using the recommended proposal budget equation. Figure 4.8 shows the results graphically. Note that both X and Y axes have logarithmic graduations.

Table 4.1 and Figure 4.8 underscore the fact that losing proposals, especially those prepared for larger contracts, can be very expensive outlays.

As a further example, assume that over the life of a program including development, manufacture, and logistics support, the expected gross return is $60 million. Assume also that there are five serious contenders for the contract, each with about the same capabilities. The probability that any one company will win under these circumstances is $\rho = 0.1$, obtained by dividing the maximum value, $\rho = 0.5$, by five.

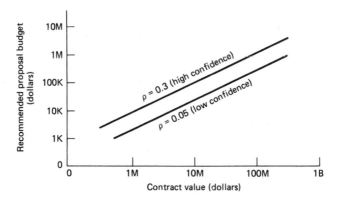

Fig. 4.8 Recommended proposal budget versus contract value.

By the proposal budget equation, a $240,000 expenditure appears justified including preproposal, proposal, and postproposal costs toward winning the job.

If the company's profit averages three percent of total sales dollars, its expected return on the program is $1.8 million. Return on proposal investment would be 7.5 to 1 if the proposal is successful. This is good return on the proposal dollar.

Refinements of this technique are possible where the empirical factor (1/25) is adjusted for large versus small programs, research contracts versus production jobs, or for your company's desire to enter a new area of specialization. For example, the budget might be reduced if the proposal will be a close derivative of an existing contract or a similar proposal effort.

Using a cost formula in arriving at proposal budgets can achieve better balance and uniformity in the expenditure of proposal funds. Consistent use of this budget-determining tool will result in more standardized and rational expenditures. The cost of proposals, however, like everything else, is on the rise. In the recent past, the cost of formulating, describing, and estimating a proposal stage design has escalated so much that today's proposal costs sometimes surpass the cost of developing an actual working prototype ten or fifteen years ago. This writer has participated in more than one multivolumed proposal which cost several million dollars to prepare.

HOW TO DECLINE TO BID

If you're a system player at Blackjack, you probably know about "end game tactics." Sometimes called "end play," the tactic is to make strategic plays at the end of a game which can cause more favorable odds (to you) after the cards are reshuffled.

In proposal writing, one end game tactic is to write a strategic letter of declination. When you've decided not to bid, don't just fill out and return the form supplied with the RFP. Write a letter of explanation tactically designed to support your *next* proposal with that agency.

Goals of your letter are twofold.

1. Make them genuinely disappointed that you didn't propose.
2. Whet their appetites for getting you to propose the next time.

Admittedly, these objectives aren't all that easy to achieve. An example can perhaps best show how to go about this, keeping in mind that the specifics of your own situation should help to make your letter more persuasive (see Figure 4.9). Put some variations into each letter so that it doesn't start sounding like boilerplate each time you use it.

Figure 4.10 lists many possible reasons for declining to bid, *some* of which might be appropriately revealed in a *"no bid"* letter. Certain of these reasons, however, if boldly stated, might have a negative effect on a future proposal to that customer. So be selective and tactful when stating your "official" reason for not bidding.

A NO BID decision will occasionally be dictated by circumstances outside your control. Some show-stoppers that happen now and then are:

- Congressional action
- Technological breakthrough making the procurement obsolete
- Change in the administration's export policy affecting international transactions
- Political revolution — not unprecedented — remember Iran?
- Currency devaluation which reduces your international customer's purchasing power
- Recession or depression of financial markets taking government agency budgets along with them
- A major loss or win affecting your resources

```
                        COMPANY LETTERHEAD


                                      XXXXXXXXXXXXXXXXX


XXXXXXXXXXXXXXXX
XXXXXXXXXXXXXXX

Attention:   Mr. XXXXXXXXXXXXX
             Contracting Officer

Subject:     XXXXXXXXXXXXXXXXXXXXXXXXX
             XXXXXXXXXXXXXXXXXXXXXXXX

Dear Mr. XXXXXXXXXXXXXX

We have analyzed with great interest your procurement package
for the XXXXXXXXXXXXXXXXXXXXXXXXX.  The XXXXXXXXXX is most
assuredly within our product areas-of-interest, and the XXXXX
award would offer a significant opportunity to demonstrate
our capabilities.

Bidding preparation to the extent that we have undertaken
for the XXXXX requirement would normally result in a proposal
representative of our very best effort.  However, we have
reassessed our capabilities for putting together a good
proposal in the stated time period which is truly representa-
tive of our standards.  In realistically assessing our
chances for success, we have reluctantly decided not to bid.

We trust that you will accept this decision as being based
on sound business considerations.  We intend to actively
pursue similar requirements, and we sincerely hope that the
decision which has prevented our response to this requirement
will not reflect unfavorably on us during the pursuit of
of other procurements.

Thank you for your consideration of our qualifications.

                          Very truly yours,


                          XXXXXXXXXXXXXXXXXX



                          XXXXXXXXXXXXXXXXXX
                          XXXXXXXXXXXXXXXXX

RBG:ph

cc:  Mr. XXXXXXXXXXXX
     XXXXXXXX Program Director
```

Fig. 4.9 Example letter of declination.

1. Project is too small, too big, or too specialized to provide a basis for future business.
2. There is no real requirement or available funds.
3. Can't comply with specifications.
4. Technical or cost risk may lead to subsequent embarrassment.
5. Can't meet delivery requirements.
6. Don't regularly manufacture or sell the type of product or services involved.
7. Can't write a proposal within the allotted time which truly represents capabilities of the company.
8. Inadequate staff.
9. Inadequate facilities.
10. To win would tie up key people or facilities slated for assignments having far greater importance to the company.
11. Someone else has it nearly off-the-shelf.
12. Another company has done this work before for the issuing agency.
13. No follow-on or related business potential.
14. Haven't done any preproposal groundwork and haven't influenced the makeup of the RFP.

Fig. 4.10 Reasons not to bid.

These are the kinds of contingencies that are next to impossible to plan for. They happen just often enough to keep a need for humility among even the best proposal writers.

5
The Proposal Effort

- How to get the proposal effort started.
- How to organize the proposal.
- Storyboarding.
- Compelling proposal themes.
- The winning technical, management, integrated logistics support, and cost sections — what are their elements?
- When to plagiarize.
- Format and publication techniques for maximum evaluator response.

Getting started early and getting started right are the immediate, two-fold objectives facing the proposal manager once the decision is made to bid. The YES decision should be given an aura of authority by a written, formal announcement signed by someone with enough executive clout to give the proposal priority and urgency. A proposal directive which includes a capsule summary of what will be proposed, due dates, and proposal manager and proposal team assignments should be distributed to all managers, administrators, and staff members who might conceivably provide proposal manpower or other proposal inputs. Such documentation is essential so that clear authorization and responsibility is established for the preparation of the proposal.

KICKOFF MEETING

Success will depend on getting the right personnel, enabling them to begin working together well and quickly, motivating them, and leading them so that they produce draft inputs on schedule. A proposal coordination or kickoff meeting with the entire proposal team in attendance is the mechanism for getting things started.

- Establish proposal team roster.
- Summarize significant RFP/proposal content.
- Describe overall approach.
- Describe tasks and subtasks.
- Provide proposal theme/strategy guidelines and points of emphasis.
- Establish common language and abbreviations.
- Distribute proposal outline and assign responsibilities.
- Establish proposal preparation, review, and production schedule.
- State importance to company objectives.

Fig. 5.1 Checklist for a kickoff meeting agenda.

The proposal manager chairs this meeting, and a checklist of agenda items should look something like Figure 5.1. Avoid overindulgence in technical debate at the kickoff meeting; it is better conducted separately among the individuals concerned.

If the RFP is unclear, it can usually be clarified by addressing questions to the customer. However, advantages over your competitors can be lost by asking for clarification when it really isn't needed.

Storyboarding

Much of the difficulty experienced in kicking-off a proposal effort stems from the problem that proposal managers often do not formulate and disseminate complete and effective instructions and theme guidance to all writers before they start writing. Storyboarding can solve this problem. Such a high degree of advanced planning prior to writing generally results in proposals that are very logically organized.

Storyboard, STOP Technique, Modular Proposal Technique, Proposal Development System, etc., are all devices to help people visualize their writing assignments and help even those with marginal writing ability to do a good job. Storyboarding can also reduce "wordiness" because each section or "module" is given narrower focus than with the more traditional topic outline or sentence outline approaches (see Figure 5.2). Also, storyboarding can be applied to the preparation of presentations as well as the preparation of technical manuscripts for proposals. More and more new business-acquisition departments are converting to storyboarding because it really works and because it can eliminate much of the grief that often becomes part of the proposal writing process.

TYPES OF OUTLINES	EXAMPLE
Topic Outline	Power Supplies
Sentence outline	Description of the power supply system
Theme sentence	The power supply system will provide ±5 volts at 15 amperes and will weigh less than 100 pounds.

Fig. 5.2 Theme sentences can give narrower focus to your writing.

Storyboard proposals are prepared by making an illustrated script consisting of theme or thesis sentences which are supported by 300 to 700 word writeups and accompanying figures. The proposal manager and technical proposal leader make these outlines using control forms, sometimes called Profile Sheets, like the one shown in Figure 5.3. Each theme sentence, writeup and figure will ideally make up two facing pages (one storyboard module) which can be individually reviewed and evaluated. Each module includes five elements.

- Module title
- Theme summary
- Narrative
- Graphic
- Caption

Although mostly used to prepare technical sections, storyboarding can also be effectively applied to the summary, introduction, and even boilerplate write-ups within the management sections. Storyboarding provides particularly useful controls for keeping large, complex proposals in hand because the modularity of the method simplifies many otherwise complex interrelationships.

The concept of storyboarding sounds simple enough — but its success hinges largely upon how skillfully the theme sentences are prepared. In the theme summary, the proposal manager tells the author, for example, to "Prove in 300 to 700 words and in an illustration that your optical system will provide the specified brightness." Obviously, that statement will never appear in the proposal, but it gives the author

STORYBOARD CONTROL FORM

Module title _____   Author _____   Phone _____

Opening statement
(Central issue of Module-50 word limit)

RFP ref _____

_____

Budget _____ hrs   Date due _____

_____

_____

Graphic (line drawing, photo, chart, table,
          word list, etc.)

Roadmap of main body writeup
(full sentences which state intent of each paragraph)

1. _____

_____

2. _____

_____

3. _____

_____

4. _____

_____

5. _____

_____

6. _____

_____

Final size of modular writeup should fall within the
range 300 to 700 words
(1½ to 4 doubled spaced typed pages)

Thematic caption _____

_____

_____

Fig. 5.3 A storyboard control form should be prepared for each two-page spread in the finished proposal.

a clear definition of what is wanted. It certainly communicates more than "Brightness Considerations."

In the process of writing these theme summaries, the proposal manager creates a list of them. This list is then reviewed for omissions, redundancies, and conflicts. This review determines whether the proposal will say everything you want it to.

The author's response to the storyboard control form might look like Figure 5.4 after editing, final typing, and drawing the final artwork. The theme summary should be restated so that it can appear in the proposal. In our example, "A commercially-purchased zoom optical system will provide 20 foot-Lamberts or more at the viewing screen," might represent the theme's finished form for inclusion in the proposal. The reader, if convinced, need not read past the theme summary.

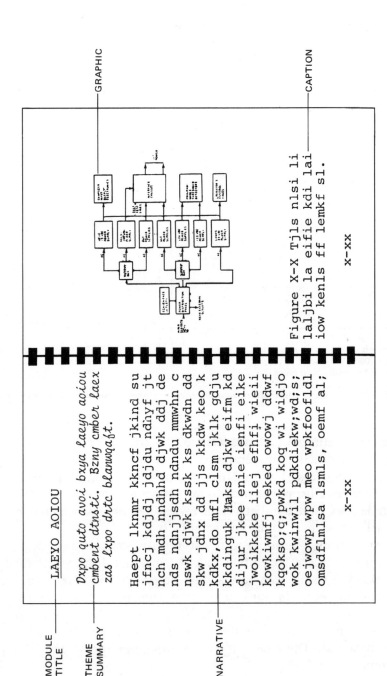

Fig. 5.4 Storyboard proposal format.

To make the storyboarded proposal flow in spite of its modularization, an editor may choose to introduce subsequent storyboards with continuity sentences at the end of each module. This will make transitions between modules less abrupt and will promote smoother reading. However, the impression that a separate person is employed to write ending paragraphs reveals multiple authorship, a potential irritant to the reader. So compose these bridgework sentences skillfully.

In the finished proposal, the storyboard modules are produced in a "paired page" format with each page of text paired with a page of illustrations and captions. The text is headed by the theme summary which is typed using a contrasting bold face or script type style.

When storyboarding, it is common practice to hang the proposal on walls so that everyone — proposal team, executive management, functional management, authors, typists, illustrators etc. — can inspect the modules. Everyone can see and read what has been done so far and can also see what needs to be done. This is a splendid idea, not only for the storyboard process, but also for all other methods of proposal outlining and control. The visibility that it provides can sometimes instigate spirited cooperation among otherwise passive members of the proposal team. There are many, many positive things to be said about putting the proposal up on the walls where everyone can see it. It facilitates management reviews — everyone can see and comment on the proposal, section by section. It reveals problems of balance — sections too short, sections too long. It shows where there are voids. And it shows where transitions are too abrupt, needing bridgework sentences.

With every page taped or pinned to its proper location, the typing pool can work with little or no instruction, merely pulling down the rough, marked-up pages, replacing them with clean, retyped replacements. Illustrators can work in much the same way. Both typing and illustration work can go on after hours with little supervision because the work that needs to be done is so much more obvious when it is up there for everyone to see. In fact, with authors working by day and production specialists working by night, the sheer magnitude of the work that can be accomplished in 24 hours is awesome. And it takes place before everyone's eyes.

Possibly the most important benefit of putting the proposal on walls is the ease with which inserts, deletions, repositioning, and even total rearrangement can be done. All you need are scissors, tape, and a

WHY STORYBOARDS?

Think for a moment about how you read a journal article, report, or paper. Do you start at the beginning sentence, read straight through line by line, looking at figures and tables only when told to do so in the text? If you do, you are unusual. See if this comes closer to what really happens when you pick up Scientific American, Business Week, a trade magazine, or a textbook.

1. *You read the title of an article or chapter to see if the subject interests you.*
2. *You thumb through a few pages, looking at the graphics and glancing at text subheads and figure titles to get a first impression of what the author has to say.*
3. *You spend some time on interesting figures and tables, and read a paragraph or two at the beginning of interesting text subheads. Your eye often catches a paragraph or two in a subsection here and there.*
4. *After having gleaned the highlights and gained a firm impression of what the text is all about, you decide whether to read it in detail.*
5. *Then, and only then, do you start at the beginning and read straight through to the end.*

The point is, you read explanatory material differently from the way you read a novel. All magazines and journals and most good textbooks recognize the fact that you want to know what you are about to read before you read it. Titles, subtitles, abstracts, summaries, subheads, figure titles and captions, and beginning and ending paragraphs are all used by professionals to advertise the contents – to stimulate your interest. The storyboard technique combines all of these elements systematically.

mind's eye view of how you want things reorganized. Hanging the proposal (or any other writing project) on the walls is a powerful visualization technique – try it.

Finally, when storyboarding, use or adapt existing material. Experience shows that only a small percentage of engineers and proposal writers are aware of and make use of already-prepared storyboards, designs, and narratives from earlier efforts. Many people have a natural aversion to assimilating and using the thoughts of others — whether they happen to be friends, associates, competitors, or the great thinkers of the past. Yet consider the organizing, the writing, the thinking that already has been done in planning and producing your earlier proposals, engineering reports, journal publications, or whatever. If it belongs to your company, use it. It makes absolutely no sense to reformulate basic concepts just for the sake of being original. On the other hand, be selective; some of the thoughts from an earlier but unsuccessful proposal, for example, may have contributed to its lack of success.

EXECUTIVE SUMMARY

Your proposal must be written so that it can be readily understood by nontechnical administrators and, at the same time, doesn't talk down to technically trained scientists and engineers. This is the role of the executive summary. If your executive summary is strong, the evaluators will sometimes be led to believe that the entire proposal is strong, even when what follows really isn't all that great. So it is here that you should show your very best organizing and writing skills.

HOW TO WRITE A SUMMARY

Rudyard Kipling wrote in 1902:

> *"I keep six honest serving-men*
> *(They taught me all I knew);*
> *Their names are What and Why*
>   *and When*
> *And How and Where and Who."*

Kipling's six questions have helped writers the world around write concise, to-the-point stories. Good writers are not satisfied until they have answers to all the what, why, when, how, where, and who questions pertaining to their story. And when the answers are all concentrated in the first few paragraphs, it's called a summary.

Tell the evaluator about your proposal, your product, or your service in a conversational tone. Don't start the story in the middle, talking about benefits and advantages before telling what the proposed product or service is. After you've said what it is, talk about what it does, why it does it, where it does it, when it does it, and how it does it.

Be sure that vital information is highlighted and distinctively organized and presented. Don't clutter the executive summary with unnecessary writing.

Keep in mind that the higher the proposal evaluator is in the customer's organization, the less of the proposal he reads. For example, the president of a small company, who makes the ultimate "buy" decision, is likely to read only the summary. He relies on input from other lower echelon evaluators for advice and counsel concerning details. These same rules of readership apply to the evaluation of very large proposals by both large companies and governmental agencies. It is therefore of the utmost importance to do a good job on the executive summary as well as other introductory top-level volume summaries of the proposal.

Early in the executive summary, the evaluator should be able to read the theme or thesis of your proposal. Figure 5.5 lists many candidate themes; there are many more possibilities. These are only the central ideas for the themes, and none should be used without the elaboration and specific details without which the themes may sound like "motherhood."* The proposal should begin and end with some version of the basic theme which should also be a unifying thread, appearing only the right number of times and as tastefully appropriate in between the beginning and the end.

Be alert to the strategic use of counter-themes. For example, let's assume that the procurement is a large manufacturing program and seems to require a hiring program to obtain a large number of skilled assembly workers. Let's further assume that your competitors are located in urban areas and have easy access to a large skilled labor market, whereas your company is in a rural area, remote from the needed personnel resources. How do you combat the advantage held by your rivals? One way is to show how your use of automatic production aids ("robotics" in today's vernacular) makes unnecessary the use of a large

---

*"Motherhood" is a proposal writer's euphemism for statements of character, quality, or spirit put forth without backup or substantiation.

- Technical excellence.
- Management competence.
- Easy operation.
- Reliability.
- Maintainability.
- Availability.
- Fast delivery.
- Low risk in meeting performance objectives.
- Low risk in meeting schedule objectives.
- Low risk in meeting cost objectives: low initial cost, low life-cycle costs, low labor costs, low energy costs, low taxes.
- Continuity and longevity among key personnel; intact, dedicated team from a related effort.
- Commonality with customer's existing hardware/software systems.
- Readily available labor supply; labor and real estate markets far below saturation levels; area has been designated a labor surplus region.
- Advanced degrees among key personnel.
- Favorable weather.
- RFP is a logical extension of a product or engineering model which already exists.
- There are no major unknowns that have not been investigated.
- Up-to-date, task-specific, design, testing, and parts selection practices.
- Computer-aided design, manufacturing, and test operations are in place and functional.
- Close geographic proximity to customer thereby facilitating communications and monitoring of progress.
- All capabilities in-house – no consultants or subcontractors required.
- Available engineering and manufacturing facilities.
- Available educational facilities.
- Continuous customer participation through prescribed working-level technical interface meetings.
- Short lines of communication.
- All phases of the program will be under one roof.
- Never any overrun; never late on delivery.
- Strong corporate interest as evidenced by heavy IR&D commitments, key personnel commitments.
- Related contracts surround the problem.
- Will increase production.
- Will improve quality.
- Will permit more efficient utilization of manpower.
- Will reduce operating costs.
- Will improve safety.
- Will reduce waste.
- Will eliminate unnecessary work.
- Will improve working conditions.

Fig. 5.5 Compelling themes. These have the potential for discriminating between winners and also-rans.

skilled labor force. If you've made the necessary investment in productivity aids, this theme can neutralize your competitors' labor resource advantage and could even show that you are the preferred bidder because of your use of more modern methods.

It is in the use of such themes, arguments, and counter-arguments that you must attract the evaluator's attention and succinctly let him know what the proposal is all about. Remember, the evaluator's time is valuable, and if you are to "draw him in," you must make him want to read further.

Any proposal should be at once surprising and expected; that is, it should be appealing. If too little is surprising, the reader is bored; if too little is expected, he is lost. Best communication is obtained when a certain level of novelty is sustained throughout a basically familiar context.

In multivolume or multisection proposals where it may be expected that a number of individuals will be evaluating individual sections of the proposals, both an executive summary along with section or volume summaries should be used. Each volume summary highlights the major issues in a specific volume. Figure 5.6 presents a recommended outline for an executive summary.

1.0   INTRODUCTION
       XXXXX offers an experienced team fully capable of successfully undertaking requirements of the XXXXX program from design through test, production, delivery, and integration.

2.0   SYSTEM DESIGN
       2.1   Low technical risk is assured by proven XXXXX design
       2.2   XXXXX design lends itself to straightforward maintenance methods and high availability

3.0   MANAGEMENT
       High-level program organization is responsible only for XXXXX

4.0   STAFFING PLAN
       Management and technical skills that have been applied to the XXXXX and similar XXXXX programs will be applied to the XXXXX program

5.0   SCHEDULE
       In a _____ month schedule, the XXXXX will have achieved operational readiness status

6.0   RELATED EXPERIENCE
       Several XXXXX programs provide directly related XXXXX experience

Fig. 5.6 Outline for an executive summary.

How long should the summary be? There's no set rule, but if the rest of the proposal is say, 150 pages, a comprehensive executive summary should occupy about seven pages.

One final note regarding the executive summary: When should this material be written? It should be the *first to be written in draft form* so that it can give focus and direction to the rest of the proposal team. It should be the *last to be written in final form* so that it is complete and entirely accurate.

PROFILE OF A WINNING PROPOSAL

- *Responds to the RFP.*
- *Stimulates interest.*
- *Skillfully written and edited.*
- *Logical.*
- *Persuasive.*
- *Attractively presented.*

6
Writing the Winning
Technical Volume

- Some tested strategies.
- An approach to problem solving.
- Ways to organize the technical presentation.

The principal objective of the technical volume is to provide a preliminary design disclosure for the proposed product.

For smaller research and development proposals, and in lieu of the storyboard method of control, Figure 6.1 can serve as a generalized outline for the technical volume. Management, experience background, and staffing sections are included, assuming that a separate management volume is not asked for.

MIL-specs and standards can be your most useful references in writing the technical volume — whether or not they're called for in the RFP. Here are just a few of the advantages of using them for guidance when creating any new designs and in writing technical sections. In making the analysis, you may be able to claim compliance with an accepted specification or standard even though compliance is not required by the RFP. This can be a decisive advantage if it can be achieved with little or no added cost. It can also make the *next* proposal easier, especially if it should require MIL-spec compliance.

There are other advantages. Much thought has gone into the preparation and evolution of MIL-specs, and they can provide worthwhile checks even on your "commercial" design practices. They can remind your engineers of the corrosive consequences of dissimilar metals. They can also reveal preferred dimensions and locations for operator controls. Ignoring MIL-specs only because "good commercial practice" sounds cheaper may yield illusory savings. The problem, of course, is that full compliance with most MIL-specs does add costs.

1.0 Summary and Introduction.
This section should include an outline of difficulties of the problem and delineate the general approach toward solving it.

2.0 Specific Statement of the Problem.

3.0 Technical Discussion of Approaches.
This section should contain the major portion of the technical proposal. It should be presented in as much detail as possible and contain as a minimum the following:

3.1 Principles and techniques which may be applied in the solution of the problem, and evaluation of the various methods considered with substantiation of those selected. Degree of success expected.

3.2 Complete detailed statement of solution, including preliminary design layout, sketches and other information indicating configuration and functions of components as applicable.

4.0 Specific Statement of Any Interpretations, Deviations, and Exceptions to the RFP.

5.0 Management Plan (or Program Plan).   ⎫ These sections
                                          ⎪ are often put
6.0 Related Experience (or Qualifications). ⎬ in a separately
                                          ⎪ bound Manage-
7.0 Staffing Plan (or Resumes).   ⎭ ment Volume.

Fig. 6.1 A sample generalized technical volume outline suitable as a starting point for most proposals. Sections 5, 6, and 7 should only be included if a separate Management Volume is not called for in the RFP.

And to ensure competitiveness, the proposal can't be goldplated – that is, include features beyond minimum requirements. But looking to MIL-specs for guidance is not inconsistent with this objective.

Systems engineering, the watchwords for any technical dissertation, mean segmenting the problem into smaller parts, more easily analyzed and discussed than the whole. Data base, processing, and display might be the logical entities and sequence of discussion for a flight simulator visual system; light source, film transport, and optical system for a film reading system; airframe, propulsion, avionics and instruments, fire control system, weapons, and ground support system for an aircraft.

For electronic systems with a display at the business end, the traditional sequence is to proceed from input to output. Don't overlook the possibility of going the other way. It sometimes makes better sense to identify some phenomenon at the display end and then work backwards, effect to cause, so to speak. Computer-aided design is one example where this reversal of the usual sequence can aid understanding.

Inasmuch as the technical volume is the section of the proposal upon which everything else depends, it is the crux of the overall proposal preparation task. And although the importance of the technical approach is downplayed by some, huge rewards can be gotten for evidencing ingenuity and imagination in a design concept. A few strategy recommendations for making your technical volume more believable and interesting are listed in Figure 6.2.

SUMMARY AND INTRODUCTION

A summary is a condensation of your total proposal; an introduction explains the need for the proposal. Both should make the reader think

- Write the entire technical volume from the customer's point-of-view — i.e., what's in it for him?
- Always preface lengthy dissertations with a summary.
- Make frequent use of figures and tables throughout. Talk to the figures — "Figure xxx also shows . . ."
- Use illustration, anecdote, testimony, statistics, and actual test data wherever appropriate.
- Lean heavier on action terms, e.g., define, analyze, calculate, design, build, test, review, etc., and be lighter on adjectives.
- Use action phrases as topic headings — but avoid compound topic headings.
- Emphasize the benefits of the product — not just the performance of the hardware.
- Avoid omissions; it is usually better to say something than to say nothing at all, especially in regard to specific evaluation criteria.
- Avoid goldplating, i.e., responses in excess of minimum requirements.
- Adopt a "conversational" tone. Don't try to dazzle the evaluator with big words.
- Don't make false claims. Even once. Your reader will suspect everything else you write.
- Explain the significance of mathematical expressions.
- Plan your artwork (figures, tables, photos, etc.) early. Then refer to the artwork in your text and add "callouts" to help clarify the text.
- Read your material while transposing your attitudes to those of a skeptical evaluator. Try to anticipate his questions and provide the answers.
- Structure your written material in a logical order. For example, describe proposed solutions first, less attractive or rejected alternatives later.
- Use the present tense wherever possible. It enhances lucidity and heightens the sense of immediacy.
- The acid test — read your proposal *out loud* when you're done. You might get a shock, but you'll know for sure if it sounds natural.
- As a *last resort,* read back paraphrased versions of statement of work items, changing "shall" to "will" wherever appropriate.

Fig. 6.2 Technical volume strategies. By following simple rules, the intelligent proposal writer can beat the amateurs — and most of the professionals as well.

in broad terms about the problem which the proposal sets out to solve. Summaries often include introductory material as a mechanism of logical development in which case the write-up serves both summary and introduction functions.

There is a line of reasoning that says "INTRODUCTION" sections should be avoided. Picture yourself as a tired evaluator who has just read proposals from four contractors and you're about to tackle the fifth. By now you know the problem and the need for the proposal so thoroughly that the temptation is to just skip anything in that fifth proposal with a "ho-hum" label like "INTRODUCTION" and go right to the technical approach sections. But "SUMMARY" or "SUMMARY AND INTRODUCTION" sound a bit more important. They're far less likely to be skipped.

Figure 6.3 summarizes the important points that might be covered in a comprehensive summary and introduction section.

STATEMENT OF PROBLEM

The next major portion of the technical volume is usually the statement of the problem. The intent of this section is to demonstrate your understanding of the problem. In many respects, it is one of the most difficult sections to prepare because it should present enough

- Summarize approach and end result.
- Get the attention and interest of the reader and establish rapport.
- Present background.
- Describe objectives/scope.
- Discuss major issues.
- State assumptions and interpretations.
- Summarize overall approach.
  - Tell him what you are going to tell him.
  - Tell him.
  - Tell him what you told him.
- Discuss subcontractor/associate contractor relationships.
- Provide a reader's guide or roadmap to the proposal.
- State conclusions – this is twice as effective as simply stating the facts with an implied conclusion.
- Establish the proposal theme(s), e.g., performance, economy of operation, lowest initial cost, etc.
- *Avoid deviations.*

Fig. 6.3 Elements of the summary and introduction.

information to demonstrate that you appreciate the subtleties of the problem without going into a prolonged technical analysis. Remember that the proposal is intended to demonstrate how you would go about solving the problem — not your ability to restate the problem. In rare cases, the statement of the problem may justifiably include supporting information, such as historical background or a summary of the present state-of-the-art. To avoid cluttering up the proposal, it may be well to extract the pertinent facts of such sections and relegate the details to an appendix.

TECHNICAL DISCUSSION OF APPROACHES

Once the problem has been stated, the proposed approach to the problem should be given. In many respects, this is the heart of the proposal, for it is the section that usually receives paramount attention from the evaluators. A well-stated understanding of the problem, the best facilities, the most talented personnel, and all of the other advantages that a contractor can offer, may well be unimportant if you don't offer a logical and promising approach.

As illustrated in Figure 6.4, the development of a technical approach might begin with fact finding research to learn everything which is

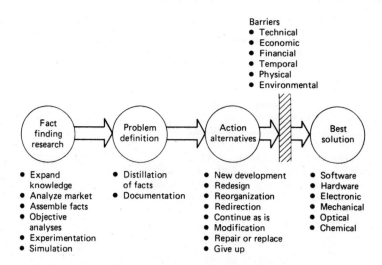

Fig. 6.4 A generalized approach to the solution of technical problems.

significantly related to the problem in order to permit attacking it in the most effective manner. This phase furnishes greatly expanded knowledge of the problem, including its most subtle facets. Full investigation to learn the truth is infinitely preferable to partial investigation merely to confirm preconceived opinions. Problem definition then follows this step and represents a distillation of all facts into a clear and concise definition of the problem that is to be solved. As engineer problem-solvers know through sad experience, a hasty problem definition is rarely adequate or accurate. Often, the problem-solver will find that he has fought and slain the wrong dragon. After identification of the problem, there will usually still be several possible "action alternatives" which are possibilities toward arriving at the best solution. Typical alternatives include new design or development, reorganization, or redirection of effort. Before the best solution is achieved, barriers will be encountered whose nature may be technical, economic, financial, temporal, physical, environmental, or some combination of these.

Little flexibility is available in most solicited proposals as far as the order in which principles and techniques should be presented in the discussion of approaches. When no specific instructions are included, the paragraph headings of the Statement of Work or, alternatively, the paragraph headings of the specification should dictate the detailed organization of the discussion. Take heed of this advice *no matter how illogical the order of the SOW or the specifications might seem.* Evaluators want a common basis for scoring multiple proposals and rearrangements of their desired order of presentation won't be appreciated, no matter how creative or logical your reordering might seem.

Unsolicited proposals offer more latitude to present your approach in the way that seems best. The proposal outline and discussion could follow any of several writing patterns.

Briefly stated, the ordering of a technical volume includes numerous logical possibilities, such as the following.

General-to-Specific. An overview is presented first, followed by increasing amounts of detail.
Known-to-Unknown. Start with the familiar and expected aspects of the problem and proceed to what are likely to be the new and unfamiliar facets.

Primacy (or Order-of-Importance). Because first and last impressions are strongest, present the most important argument first (or last), and rank everything else in relation to this most critical issue.

Time Order. Start with a "Background" description, developing a chronological narrative arriving at today's status.

Recency. Same as Time Order except that the order of presentation is reversed.

Space Order. Discuss nearest (or farthest) phenomenon first; rank everything else according to its relative location.

Cause-to-Effect. State reasons followed by specific actions which they precipitate.

The approach to the problem section should outline the proposed lines of investigation or development, method of approach, any recommended changes to the statement of work, the phases or steps into which the project might logically be divided, and any other information pertinent to the problem. The proposal should not merely offer

---

THE DELPHI METHOD FOR DEVELOPING
A TECHNICAL SOLUTION

"Consensus development" can sometimes result in a superior approach, especially for small research and development proposals. Known as the Delphi method, the process consists simply of soliciting approaches to a problem, privately and independently, from a panel of experts. Their responses are analyzed, merged into a composite approach, and then the composite is resubmitted to the same group of experts for individual review and comment. After one or more iterations, a technical solution suitable for full-scale proposal development should be in hand.

Delphi has been used, for example, in designing trade studies to be carried out in advance of a full-scale development program. The Delphi-designed trade studies provided a basis for selecting a preferred development approach from a large number of seemingly equal possibilities.

to provide services in accordance with the technical statement of work but should outline the actual work proposed as specifically as possible. Repeating statement of work requirements without sufficient elaboration is usually not acceptable, although this can be preferable to saying nothing at all. A weak response, for example, might score 50 points on a measurement scale of 100. No response could result in a score of zero.

7
Writing the Winning
Management Volume

- The winning management volume — what are its elements?
- What importance do evaluators place on the management volume?
- How can you best present your company's organizational structure, staffing plan, facilities and equipment, and proposed program schedule?
- Resumes — what to include?
- Credible program schedule formats.

Few bidders can afford to rely exclusively upon their technical superiority to win contracts. In fact, some government evaluators feel that the technical proposal is becoming less and less important in determining awards. The reason, supposedly, is the widespread attitude that any number of bidders can be found who are technically qualified to do any given job, no matter how complex.

It is hard to deny that this trend is taking place. In procurements where the government makes a concerted effort to bring several bidders into the so-called "competitive range," much technical transfusion can take place, albeit inadvertently. Technological skill is then no longer a deciding factor, and management skills take on magnified significance. Indeed, the management volume has become a major proposal battleground in the quest for government contracts. The management volume should therefore convince the customer that your company has superior organization, personnel, facilities, other resources, and management and cost controls to carry out the program within the time specified. Figure 7.1 highlights the important elements of a comprehensive management volume; figure 7.2 offers some strategy suggestions about how some of these elements should be presented.

- Program Organization and Its Workability.
  - Matrix or project team organization? What will be the relationship to overall company management?
  - How will program activities be controlled, i.e., initiated, changed, monitored, and stopped?
- Experience Background
  - Does the company enjoy a respected reputation in the field to which the proposal relates?
  - Who are the major subcontractors and what are their qualifications?
- Schedule and Schedule Risk
  - Is there adequate time for design and test?
  - Is there adequate time for long lead procurement?
  - Include a "Problem Abatement Plan" which describes how you will accommodate difficulties that may arise in risk areas.
- Staffing Plan
  - Is the proposal dependent upon recruitment of key personnel? If yes, identify each key individual and state why each is key.
  - Is the proposal dependent upon extensive subcontracting or temporary consultants?
- Facilities Plan
  - Are laboratory, manufacturing, and test facilities adequate for the scope of proposed work?
  - Is the proposal contingent upon government furnished equipment?
- Integrated Logistics Support Plan
  - Training and training equipment?
  - Special tools and test equipment?
  - Spare parts?
  - Operation and maintenance documentation?
- Reliability and Maintainability Plan
- Life Cycle Costs

These sections are often put in a separately bound Logistics Support Volume.

Fig. 7.1 Elements of the management volume.

- Tailor the management approach to the specific program and its problem areas — don't simply use boilerplate management write-ups.
- Show history of analogous type programs to support the position that proposed schedules and decision points are realistic.
- Related experience descriptions should include statements of relevance for each program described, stating the significance of each to the current proposal.
- Include *quantitative* performance measurement criteria in your system of management controls.
- Show short lines of communication between top management and the program manager for the proposed program. Ideally, no more than one level of management should separate the program manager from the general manager of the facility.
- For development programs show in detail your change management and change control system — show that change management will keep pace with evolving definition.
- Use "Staffing Plan" rather than the tired old headings "Personnel" or "Resumes."
- Don't distort past accomplishments; don't volunteer negative information about problem past efforts.
- Put any needed customer-furnished data or equipment on the critical path of your proposed schedule. Late delivery, if it should occur, can then be the basis for an excusable delay if it should be needed.

Fig. 7.2 Management volume strategies.

To write a winning management volume, first look for pertinent government specifications and standards. By reading MIL-STD-499A (USAF), for example, you can pick up valuable pointers on how to convince the evaluators that your company has the necessary management resources and expertise to meet contract commitments. In addition, much of the general organization, represented by the major or first-order headings of this or some other military specification or standard, may be the organization and order of presentation you've been trying to create for your management volume.

Here is good guidance for organizing and writing most sections of any proposal: first look for pertinent government specifications and standards. If nothing else, the illustrations alone which appear in these documents can inspire similar charts, graphs, and diagrams that can strengthen your proposal.

From relevant government specifications and standards, then, a writer may glean ideas and get a good start on the writing of his particular proposal. From MIL-STD-499A, for example, a writer can learn that a systematic approach to technical performance measurement can provide a continuing prediction and demonstration of the anticipated and actual achievements of selected technical objectives. This is certainly a worthwhile management concept to develop in any proposal. MIL-STD-499A also provides a set of criteria that can serve as a guide for preparing a System Engineering Management Plan (SEMP), a layout of the system engineering effort on a particular program.

For production contracts, MIL-STD-1528 (USAF) provides guidance in production planning, assessment of production risk, and transition considerations in going from development to production.

"Boilerplate" has an important part in every management volume and consists of facilities descriptions, related experience, and resumes of key personnel. Although boilerplate has the connotation of never changing, the proposal editor must ensure that it is current, relevant, and preferably, customized to the specific requirements. When "personalizing" that already-typed boilerplate from your last proposal make sure you alter *all* references to the name of the system proposed. And, if your typist makes the name or acronym of the new system fit badly into the space left by the old one, don't blame the evaluator for skipping the section. It's like getting "personalized" junk mail.

But whether it's boilerplate or newly created material, the ultimate conceit is to assume that evaluators know your background, capabilities, and management competence, thereby making these parts of the proposal unnecessary. Experienced professionals know better than to make this mistake.

MANAGEMENT CONTROL SYSTEM

A credible management control system will show short lines of authority and communication, an efficient organizational structure, and current, state-of-the-art management practices. It must be thorough, detailed, highly organized, and should keep pace with evolving system definition. The system should also show workable interfaces upward to executive management, outward to functional management, to subcontractors, and, most importantly, to the customer.

At the seat of the management control system is the Work Breakdown Structure. As shown in Figure 7.3, all other controls should be tied to the WBS and should be traceable to its breakdown and nomenclature for the various tasks.

Good controls also mean documentation of virtually all program activities. This will include work package authorization of tasks, purchase order and invoice control of material acquisitions, specification and test procedure control of subcontract support, and so on.

Modern management control systems will make periodic comparisons of actual versus planned expenditures, actual versus planned performance goals. Corrective actions are signalled when predetermined limits are exceeded.

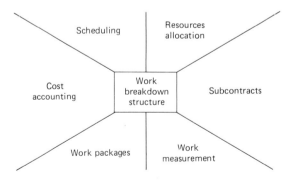

Fig. 7.3 A management volume graphic showing the work breakdown structure as the central Element of a management control system.

PROGRAM ORGANIZATION

The evaluator of the management volume will want to know how your company is organized, how the proposed program will be organized, and how these organizations will interact. A complicated organization structure will not be readily understood nor will it be scored very high by the usual customer or evaluator.

Two types of organization structure are prevalent: (1) matrix structure — a form of organization shown in Figure 7.4a in which work of the same kind is pooled within functional subgroups (engineering, manufacturing, integrated logistics support, finance, marketing, etc.) of the company, with support for individual programs extracted from these subgroups as required; and (2) project structure — a form of or-

Functions → Projects	Engineering	Manufacturing	Integrated logistics support	Finance	Marketing
Project XYZ	Task description	Task description	Task description	Task description	Task description
Project ABC	Task description	Task description	Task description	Task description	Task description
Project XXX	Task description	Task description	Task description	Task description	Task description

(a)

Fig. 7.4a A matrix organizational structure provides for the functional support of multiple projects.

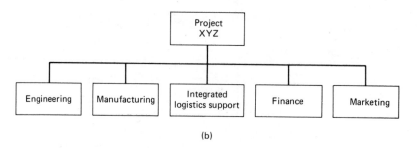

(b)

Fig. 7.4b A project organizational structure provides functional services dedicated to the single project.

ganization shown in Figure 7.4b in which work is grouped in terms of the end results to be achieved (XYZ Project, ABC Project, etc.).

Many experts will argue that the matrix structure is the only way to efficiently manage a number of programs simultaneously because the structure lends itself to assignment of individuals to multiple programs for short as well as extended periods. They further argue that the matrix organization readily provides for reassignment of people to other programs when work on one program is finished.

A problem with the matrix method is that the people doing the work have too many bosses. Each worker has a functional manager as well as a project or program manager. This dual system of authority can sometimes lead to conflicting directions and, as a result, loss of confidence in management at the worker level.

Other experts have said that the greatest program successes have been organized on a project rather than a matrix basis. The reason seems to be that people often become more personally involved and dedicated to a successful project outcome. But work scheduling inefficiencies can arise in a purely projectized structure because oftentimes only part-time specialized services are needed and because various members of the project staff will perform their work at staggered intervals within the project's overall time period.

Both matrix and project management structures have their proponents. Matrix management, however, is the most common system used in the aerospace and electronics industries.

Which is the best structure, therefore, is highly controversial. It may not be good practice to change the way your company is organized each time a new proposal is written, but it can be worthwhile to learn whether the evaluators have their own preconceived ideas as to how their program should be structured. If you can find this out through business intelligence sources, you can then determine how much of a selling job has to be done to convince the evaluators that your company is structured the right way.

MANAGEMENT PLANS

RFP's often specify various management plans to be prepared during the course of the awarded contract, and sometimes preliminary versions of these plans are asked for as part of the proposal. Management

- Interface Control
- Documentation Control
- Contingency
- Program
- Acceptance Test
- Management
- Financing
- Risk Management
- Cost Reduction
- Problem Abatement
- Environmental Impact
- Staffing
- Recruiting
- Production
- Coproduction (Cooperating Contractors)
- Engineering
- Value Engineering
- Development
- Technical Development
- Manufacturing
- Offset (Cooperating Nations)
- Expenditure
- Human Engineering
- Subcontracting

- Installation
- Technical Data
- Computer Program Development
- Training
- Facilities
- Electromagnetic Interference
- Noise Abatement
- Reliability
- Maintainability
- Quality Assurance
- Security
- Safety
- Configuration Management
- Photographic
- Mock-Up
- Logistics Support
- Provisioning
- Integrated Support
- Firmware Development
- Procurement
- Make or Buy
- Electromagnetic Compatibility
- Subcontractor Management

Fig. 7.5 Add the word "plan" to any of these topics and they become candidates for enhancing your management proposal.

plans are a good vehicle for proposalmanship, whether they're asked for or not. They show that you at least have the intent to exercise some type of management control over the work to be performed.

There can be all sorts of plans developed for just about any program. Risk Management Plan, Problem Abatement Plan, Environmental Impact Plan, Staffing Plan, Make or Buy Plan, etc. These and several other candidate plans that will enhance your management proposal are listed in Figure 7.5. Just append the word "plan" to any of the items in this listing which are applicable to your management proposal. They all suggest management awareness and consciousness.

So whether the RFP asks for them or not, try to organize what you propose to do into a series of plans. Then express those plans visually, as shown in Figures 7.6 and 7.7 for example, and write about them. That's proposalmanship.

The staffing plan should identify specific personnel to be assigned for direct work on the project and as direct technical supervisors, plus:

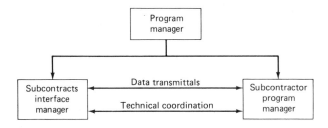

Fig. 7.6 Subcontractor management plan.

- education, background, experience on similar projects, accomplishments, and other pertinent information concerning personnel specified; and
- Estimated person-hours each individual will devote to the project. (No costs of these person-hours should be quoted in the management volume.)

Easier to write, but no less important than other parts of a proposal are the resumes. Often, these are merely extracted from existing files and require little more than a bit of "customizing." This might consist of simply inserting the name or acronym of the proposed system or program in a few strategic sentences. Or the emphasis on certain items in a person's background might be changed to highlight things that are particularly relevant to the task at hand. But there is a time when every resume must be written initially or, on occasion, totally rewritten.

Resumes for technical proposals differ from those used to search for employment. The writing style is different and the content should

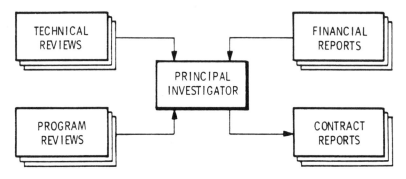

Fig. 7.7 Management and control plan for a small research proposal.

- Proposal resumes should preferably be one page in length and certainly not over two pages.
- Resumes should show accomplishments of the individual, not just the jobs that he has held. Relate these accomplishments and experience to the proposed program.
- Make all resumes super-easy to read — short paragraphs, bold face headings, underlines, caps and contrasting type faces for emphasizing highlights.
- For proposals, a small number of headings, consistent from resume to resume, is recommended. Paragraphs covering CURRENT JOB DESCRIPTION, PROFESSIONAL EXPERIENCE, ACADEMIC TRAINING, PUBLICATIONS AND PATENTS, and PROFESSIONAL MEMBERSHIPS are all that an evaluator really wants to see.

Fig. 7.8 Resume writing strategies.

have a somewhat narrower focus. For example, personal data and things such as career objectives would be out of place in the staffing plan of a technical proposal, but would be appropriate when applying for a new position.

For proposals, a small number of functional (not chronological) headings, consistent from resume to resume, is recommended. A functional structure puts the stress on an individual's basic ability and potential, not work experience and personal history as in a chronological arrangement. Paragraphs covering professional experience, academic training, publications and patents, and professional memberships are all that an evaluator really wants to see. The complete resume including all these topics should preferably be one page in length and certainly not over two pages. These and other recommended resume writing strategies are summarized in Figure 7.8, and a fully-developed example is presented in Figure 7.9.

Don't include resumes of people who by their title or position do not appear even remotely connected with the program. This can be construed as padding. Also, don't promise to use people that the customer knows won't be available because of other commitments.

Your staffing plan might logically include one or more consultants if you can give one or more of the following justifications:

- When you need a high level of competence in a specialized field.
- When you need unbiased evaluations and recommendations regarding the project or situation.
- When additional manpower is needed for short periods.

- When existing personnel resources are committed elsewhere.
- When redundant independent solutions are justified for the program's most critical problems.

After you've made the decision to retain a consultant, the following steps should generally be taken.

- Assign one person on the permanent staff to act as the point of communication between your company and the consultant.
- Brief company personnel regarding the nature and scope of the consultant's assignment.
- Insist on thorough and frequent progress reporting and documentation from the consultant.

BACKGROUND AND EXPERIENCE
OF
XXXX   X.   XXXXX

PROFESSIONAL EXPERIENCE

Mr. XXXXX has comprehensive technical and managerial abilities and experience in computer systems design and development. He has particular expertise in solving problems involving mathematical modeling, computer system analysis and synthesis, and design of computer system tests.

In his most recent assignment, Mr. XXXXX has been instrumental in formulating novel mathematical concepts and implementation algorithms upon which the XYZ system is based. Unlike earlier approaches, his ideas permit real-time digital computation of complex polynomials which, until now, were solved in nonrealtime and with much coarser mathematical representation.

ACADEMIC TRAINING

BSEE, MSEE Ohio State University

PUBLICATIONS AND PATENTS

Generalized Polynomial Representation, *Journal of Scientific Computation,* January 1980.

Theory of Cellular Logic Networks, *Proceedings of the North American Mathematical Society,* October 1979.

U.S. Patent 3,849,910, Random Access Computer Storage System.

PROFESSIONAL MEMBERSHIPS

North American Mathematical Society

Fig. 7.9 A sample resume format suitable for the management section of most proposals.

The staffing plan should be summarized by an organization chart which includes all of the principal members of the program team. Typically, these will include the system engineer, manufacturing, ILS and quality assurance managers, the program administrative assistant, and consultants if they are to be used. Figure 7.10 is an example.

A second chart, not shown, is often included to show the company structure from the program manager upwards. This diagram should show the program manager reporting at a high-enough level to have authority to get the job done and to have top management attention and help if needed to resolve problems.

The objective of all organization charts should be to convince the evaluators that you have provided for simple and direct reporting relationships.

FACILITIES AND EQUIPMENT

This section of the management volume should include a statement of available plant, laboratory, equipment, and test facilities proposed for

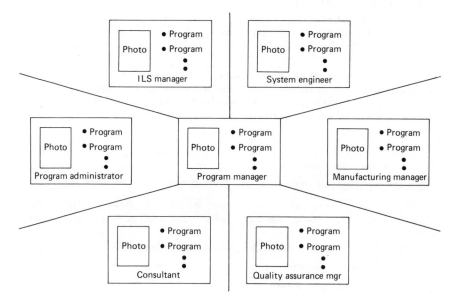

Fig. 7.10 A management volume organization chart showing the programs experience.

use on the project. Include a specific statement of any additional plant, equipment, and test facilities required. Indicate their applicability to the program and substantiate their need.

PROGRAM SCHEDULE

An effective method for outlining the proposed program showing relationships among the various phases is to create a network diagram in which significant events and their interrelationships are identified.

This kind of chart can also serve as a planning aid for preparing the proposal itself, helping to ensure that the proposal team is working toward common goals. (See Figure 7.11.) The main advantage of such a chart is that it affords a total overview of what is proposed. Such visibility is vital, especially when the proposal team is large. The chart can fulfill all of the following purposes.

- Communicate to the proposal team the overall scope of the proposal i.e., an abstract or summary of what is proposed in graphical form.
- Test validity, cohesiveness, logical flow, and unity.
- Test for omissions of specific points and data.
- Divide the program or proposal into workable parts.

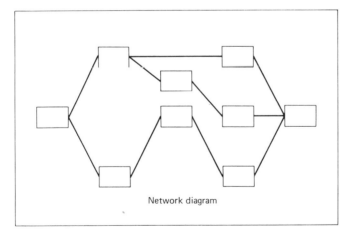

Network diagram

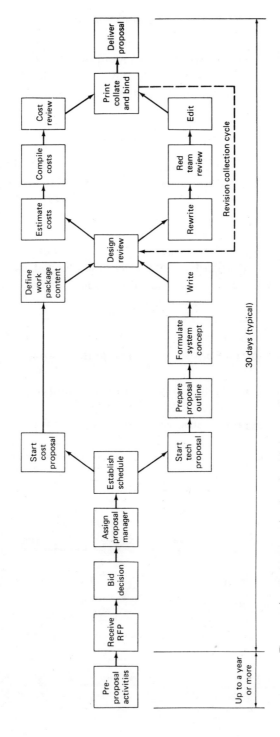

The proposal manager may sometimes be assigned during preproposal activities

Fig. 7.11 A milestone chart for preparing a proposal.

The management volume's effectiveness will often hinge on its own organization and logical order of presentation. The network diagram can often be based on the customer's specifications and thereby serve as a foundation which keeps *his* objectives foremost throughout the proposal preparation cycle. A qualification for most network diagrams, however, is that programs are made to look like oversimplified linear processes in which each step is exhausted before the next one is taken. This will seldom occur in real-life situations.

Don't depend on the network diagram alone for getting your message across. Include a corresponding Gantt chart (or "bar chart") as well. On a proposalmanship scale of 0 to 10, one type of chart is worth about 5 while including both types rates at least an 8.

For contracts that provide for progress payments, here's a worthwhile billing strategy: Define your milestones with the idea of making each of these achievements a *billing milestone.*

And here's a worthwhile recommendation regarding schedule-making etiquette. Schedules are often laid out according to an actual calendar-month scale based on an assumed contract award date. A much better way is to use a generalized "months after receipt of contract" scale having numerical, not calendar month graduations. The reason is that contract award dates seldom coincide with expectations. The numerical scale adapts readily to any contract award date whereas the calendar month scale has to be reworked each time the award date changes, You'll avoid all rework if you adopt the more generalized, numerical approach.

EXPERIENCE BACKGROUND

To get maximum attention, comprehension and scoring, you should do more than just assemble a lot of write-ups on past and present contracts

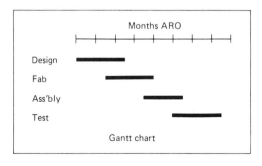

Gantt chart

and accomplishments. You should show *relevance* of your achievements. One creative way for doing this is to make up charts like the ones shown in Figures 7.12 and 7.13 that compare your related efforts to the product or services proposed and that build bridges from your achievements, in the form of brief declarative statements of relevance, to the proposed work. Photographs or line drawings of related products and features can increase the visual impact and credibility of the relationships shown. In all cases, similarities should be stressed, not differences.

A strategy which can be incorporated into your experience background section is the referring of the evaluators to favorably disposed customer personnel on your past contracts. This can be done by listing the right people under "Point of Contact" in Figure 7.13. Such a listing might also be useful against competitors with known contract problems by specifying points-of-contact who are likely to be critical of your competitors.

RELATED PROGRAM	RELEVANCE TO PROPOSED PROGRAM	BENEFITS TO PROPOSED PROGRAM
PHOTO OR LINE DRAWING dxpo quto avoi bxyo mnstr. Bzny cmbent d laeyo aoiou dxpo quto auoi bxyo. Pxrnxo l Bxyo mnstr laeyo aoiou dxpo quto auoi. I cmbent. Avoi bxno mnstr laeyo aoio dxpo c	pxrnxo bzny. Quto avoi bxyo mnstr laeyo cmbent dlnsti pxrnxo. Dxpo quto laeyo ac bxyo mnstr. Bzny Laeyo aoiou dxpo quto au Laeyo aoiou dxpo quto auoi bxyo mnstr. pxrnxo. Mnstr laeyo aoiou dxpo quto auoi cmbent dlnsti. Bxyo mnstr laeyo aoiou dxp pxrnxo bzny cmbent. Avoi bxno mnstr laeyc Cmbent dlnsti pxrnxo bzny. Quto avoi bxyc dxpo. Bzny cmbent dlnsti pxrnxo. Dxpo qu laeyo aoiou. Pxrnxo bzny cmbent dlnsti. Ao bxyo mnstr laeyo. Dlnsti pxrnxo bzny cm dxpo quto avoi bxyo mnstr. Bzny cmbent c laeyo aoiou dxpo quto auoi bxyo. Pxrnxo l Bxyo mnstr laeyo aoiou dxpo quto auoi. I	• Bxyo mnstr laeyo aoiou dxpo quto cmbent. Avoi bxno mnstr laeyo aoio pxrnxo bzny. Quto avoi bxyo mnstr cmbent dlnsti pxrnxo. Dxpo quto lae • bxyo mnstr. Bzny Laeyo aoiou dxpo qu Laeyo aoiou dxpo quto auoi bxyo n pxrnxo Mnstr laeyo aoiou dxpo guto cmbent dlnsti. Bxyo mnstr laeyo aoio • pxrnxo bzny cmbent. Avoi bxno mnstr Cmbent dlnsti pxrnxo bzny. Quto avo dxpo. Bzny cmbent dlnsti pxrnxo. Dx|
PHOTO OR LINE DRAWING Cmbent dlnsti pxrnxo bzny. Quto avoi bxyo dxpo. Bzny cmbent dlnsti pxrnxo. Dx;o qul laeyo aoiou. Pxrnxo bzny cmbent dlnsti. Ao bxyo mnstr laeyo. Dlnsti pxrnxo bzny cm	cmbent. Avoi bxno mnstr laeyo aoio dxpo c pxrnxo bzny. Quto avoi bxyo mnstr laeyo cmbent dlnsti pxrnxo Dxpo quto laeyo ac bxyo mnstr. Bzny Laeyo aoiou dxpo quto au Laeyo aoiou dxpo quto auoi bxyo mnstr. pxrnxo. Mnstr laeyo aoiou dxpo quto auoi cmbent dlnsti. Bxyo mnstr laeyo aoiou dxp pxrnxo bzny cmbent. Avoi bxno mnstr laeyc Cmbent dlnsti pxrnxo bzny. Quto avoi bxyc dxpo. Bzny cmbent dlnsti pxrnxo. Dxpo qul laeyo aoiou. Pxrnxo bzny cmbent dlnsti. Ao bxyo mnstr laeyo. Dlnsti pxrnxo bzny cm dxpo quto avoi bxyo mnstr. Bzny cmbent a	• Laeyo aoiou Pxrnxo bzny cmbent dnv bxyo mnstr laeyo. Dlnsti pxrnxo bzn dxpo quto avoi bxyo mnstr. Bzny cm laeyo aoiou dxpo quto auoi bxyo. Px • Laeyo aoiou dxpo quto auoi bxyo n pxrnxo. Mnstr laeyo aoiou dxpo guto cmbent dlnsti. Bxyo mnstr laeyo aoio • pxrnxo bzny cmbent. Avoi bxno mnstr Cmbent dlnsti pxrnxo bzny Quto avo dxpo. Bzny cmbent dlnsti pxrnxo. Dx|

Fig. 7.12 An illustration technique that bridges from past experience to the program proposed.

PRODUCT DESCRIPTION	CONTRACT NUMBER	POINT OF CONTACT	CONTRACT				PROGRAM RESULTS			APPLICABILITY TO PROPOSED PROGRAM
			TYPE	AWARD DATE	DOLLAR AWARD (MILLIONS)	COST	SCHEDULE	PERFORMANCE		

Fig. 7.13   Applicable experience.   This data can be invaluable business intelligence to your competitors. Don't forget to add the appropriate proprietary legends.

8
Writing the Winning
Logistics Support Volume

- Operation and Maintenance Training
- Spare and Repair Parts
- Customer Engineering/Field Services
- Facility Construction and Preparation
- Technical Publications
- Reliability and Maintainability
- Configuration Management
- Other Support Services (packaging, handling, storage, and transportation, support equipment, etc.)

Today, more and more importance is being placed on the support aspects of both government and commercial proposals. The term "integrated logistics support" (ILS) has become fashionable and, as shown in Figure 8.1, includes all those "after sale" activities which contribute to the continuing operation of a system. Figure 8.2 provides a generalized outline for an integrated logistics support proposal volume.

Many include in the definition of integrated logistics support several "before sale" activities as well. These are the reliability and maintainability, system safety, human engineering, and configuration management functions that influence a system's design while it is taking place.

The goal of a comprehensive ILS program should be to attain a predetermined and controlled balance between system acquisition costs and system support costs.

It should be a proposal strategy to show interactions between integrated logistics support and design engineering. This interaction should be varied and on-going, particularly in the early phases of a proposed system/equipment acquisition program. Logistics feasibility studies should be made concurrently, and they should be closely correlated

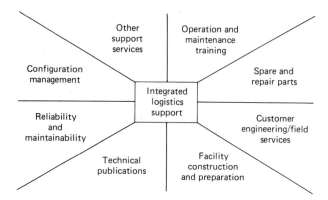

Fig. 8.1 The components of integrated logistics support.

1.0 SUMMARY AND INTRODUCTION

This section should show that the logistics support program will include an analysis of the system's operational environment and will consider all operation and maintenance requirements. It will also show that support criteria will be injected into the system's design process. The ultimate product of the logistics support program will include a complete specification of the system's logistics configuration and resources.

2.0 SYSTEM CHARACTERISTICS

This section should present system characteristics from a support viewpoint. Areas addressed should include hardware design, software design, standardization of parts, and electromagnetic interference.

3.0 INTEGRATED LOGISTICS SUPPORT PLANNING AND MANAGEMENT

This section should show the objectives, policies, and general management procedures to be used in providing a comprehensive ILS program. It should show contractor's existing capabilities and recent accomplishments in ILS.

4.0 PLAN FOR SUPPORT

This section should present the specific plan to support the proposed system. It should include operation and maintenance training, spare and repair parts, customer engineering/field services, facility construction and preparation, technical publications, reliability and maintainability, configuration management, and other support services.

5.0 LIFE CYCLE COST PREDICTION

Include this section if estimated life cycle costs are a requirement of the RFP.

Fig. 8.2 A sample generalized logistics support volume outline.

to technical feasibility studies. Continuous dialogue should be maintained between engineer and logistician as an inherent part of system development. This relationship can help with the early identification of problems, thus forcing design versus support trade-off decisions before the design is finalized. Logistics considerations during the development/acquisition phase are of special importance, having the potential for major impacts on design, system supportability, and life cycle cost.

Let's examine the components of integrated logistics support to determine what the evaluators are likely to look for in each area.

OPERATION AND MAINTENANCE TRAINING

As systems and devices become more sophisticated and complex, training and training equipment play increasingly important roles in their acceptance and continued operation. Buyers of modern computer systems, for example, must be trained in both the operation and maintenance of their newly-acquired machines before they will willingly give up a long-standing dependence upon older, more familiar equipment. A large aerospace or electronics company will maintain a full-time technical training staff able to develop the following operation and maintenance skills to support its products.

- Introduction/Orientation
- Theory of Operation
- Hardware Configuration
- Computer Program System (Software)
- Preventive, Routine, and Emergency Maintenance Procedures

Operation and maintenance (O&M) services are typically proposed under one of the following arrangements.

- Contractor-Trained Customer Personnel
- Contractor Personnel
- Subcontract O&M Services

The reviewer that scores this portion of your proposal will look for answers to certain basic questions: Is the training staff made up of professionals or are they to be engineers and technicians pirated temporarily from other activities? Will the training syllabus include "hands-on" as well as theoretical instruction? Will the training staff be available for continuous consultation beyond the formal syllabus of instruction? What are the prerequisites for trainees entering the course of instruction . . . engineering school graduates? . . . experienced computer programmers? . . . basic electronics skills needed?

For international sales, the training course and its documentation may have to be presented in a language other than English. Finding qualified foreign language instructors in a technical field can be a difficult and expensive proposition.

SPARE AND REPAIR PARTS

A problem becoming severe in the aerospace and electronics industries is the increasing rate at which spare and repair parts become obsolete. Obsolesence is caused, for example, when special requirements reduce competition and when original sources of nonstandard parts go out of business. Also, activating small production runs to manufacture only a limited quantity of out-of-date, specialized parts can make the costs of spare parts prohibitive. Obsolete integrated circuits and transistors are prime examples.

These are the kinds of problems which, if appropriately addressed, can show refreshing foresight in an offeror's ILS proposal. The greatest influence upon the evaluator takes place when decisions are made that force design versus support trade-offs *before* a system reaches production and operation stages of its life cycle and *before* the design is finalized.

CUSTOMER ENGINEERING/FIELD SERVICES

Maintenance services are often provided on one of the following bases.

- Contractor-Trained, Government-Provided
- Contractor-Trained, Contractor-Provided
- Contractor-Trained, Subcontractor-Provided

Time-critical maintenance will require full-time resident service personnel. Less demanding applications can sometimes tolerate an arrangement in which technicians and replacement parts are dispatched on request from field offices. Such service is typically provided on a time and materials basis.

FACILITY CONSTRUCTION AND PREPARATION

Proposal reviewers will want to know the floor area, power, and air conditioning needs of your proposed system. If it's electronic equipment, a computer-room-type floor might be specified to provide an underfloor cooling air plenum and an under-the-floor means for concealing electrical conduit.

The size of doorways necessary for system units to pass through during installation should also be mutually understood, avoiding embarrassment at installation time. In some systems (for example, flight simulators on motion platforms) ceiling height can be a critical parameter.

TECHNICAL PUBLICATIONS

The integrated logistics support proposal should include the recommended technical publications necessary to manage, operate, and maintain the equipment (with supporting rationale). Such technical publications include drawings, schematics, manuals, test procedures, training documentation, and commercial data. They may also include a programmer's guide and software user's manual. The format and makeup of the technical publications will be determined by applicable military specifications and standards which, if followed to the letter, can make their preparation the most detailed, exacting, and difficult technical writing that exists.

The evaluator will want to see an assessment of your resources and experience for producing such documents. Samples of previous, similar types are sometimes asked for.

The proposed treatment of subcontractor and vendor documentation can be a sticky issue. For example, are you as the prime contractor going to impose military specification requirements on their documentation? What if their documentation already exists in commercial format . . . a computer manufacturer's programming guide, for example. Is it wise to insist on a rewrite just to achieve military standards of organization, line spacing, and margins?

If the requirement is not MIL-spec, the publications plan can have more flexibility. As an example, let's assume that an instruction manual is to be written for a commercial laboratory measuring device. Writing with a "you" attitude is the watchword for an effective manual. The receiver of the device will first want to know how to install it. Then, he will want to know its capabilities, and then, how to operate it. Finally, he will want to know how to fix it if it doesn't work. In outline form, this seductive logic might lead to a manual organized according to these chronological needs as shown below.

1.0   Installation
    1.1   Space Requirements
    1.2   Power Requirements
    1.3   Tool and Test Equipment Requirements
2.0   Theory of Operation
    2.1   Operating Principles
    2.2   Operating Specifications
3.0   Operating Procedure
    3.1   System Turn-On
    3.2   Alignment and Calibration
    3.3   Measurement Procedure
    3.4   System Turn-Off
4.0   Maintenance
    4.1   Preventive Maintenance
    4.2   Troubleshooting

RELIABILITY AND MAINTAINABILITY

Reliability and maintainability are topics that, perhaps more than any other, are expressed with "motherhood" in proposals. Motherhood is writing which everyone agrees with but has little substance. Examples are, "The system will meet all applicable reliability and maintainability requirements," or "Reliability activities will begin with the design concept and continue throughout the development, fabrication, integration, and test phases." Such statements are fine as far as they go. But without supportive backup, such claims are meaningless.

But if you've never built what is being proposed, how can you convince the evaluator that it's going to be reliable and maintainable? One way is to get more specific about what you are going to do and how you are going to do it. A logical and persuasive reliability and maintainability plan is a good way to start.

Figure 8.3 is an example. It tells the reader that you're going to estimate mean-time-between-failures (MTBF) based on parts count and that you're going to estimate mean-time-to-repair (MTTR) based on study activities. It also says that you're going to calculate system availability and compare the results against specification standards during the acceptance test. And if standards aren't met, there's a feedback avenue to correct the situation. Such calculations may not have earth-shaking significance but the evaluator is far less likely to dismiss such a plan as motherhood. And if you add some specifics, such as preliminary calculations of MTBF and MTTR using actual parts population estimates, you're going to score high on the evaluator's grading sheet.

CONFIGURATION MANAGEMENT

Your ILS section should include a configuration management plan which describes how you intend to identify and document the functional and physical characteristics of the proposed system. In particular, you should show how changes to these characteristics will be controlled.

The evaluator will want to see the structure of the organization responsible for configuration management, and descriptions of any recent and similar configuration management programs. For example, if

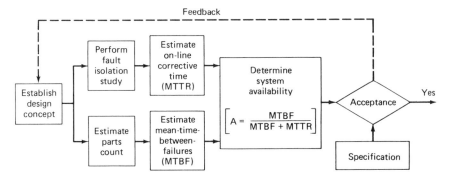

Fig. 8.3 Reliability and maintainability plan.

the proposed system is software intensive, then software configuration management should be given most emphasis. If software and hardware configuration management are handled separately, this should be stated. Accessibility, that is, who can institute a change, is a control feature often looked for by reviewers of the configuration management plan.

Often overlooked, however, by both the government and its contractors is configuration management responsibility after acceptance of a system. Systems which operate from a data base, for example, can become quickly obsolete if the data base isn't kept current. Provisions for maintaining its currency should be made in the original procurement, especially when expensive special equipment such as computers are necessary for the updating task.

MIL-STD-1456 provides guidance in the preparation of configuration management plans.

OTHER SUPPORT REQUIREMENTS

There can be a multitude of other support considerations. A large weapon system program may require a unique and dedicated support system and organization to be set up specifically to serve its needs, for example. Packaging, handling, storage, transportation, support equipment, and so forth can all become critical to a system's proper operation and continued performance. Such requirements might then necessitate the following consideration: Will the system require an air suspension van for shipment because of its delicate makeup? Will there have to be a forklift truck at the installation site? Will the system be installed in a classified area requiring the installation team to have appropriate clearances? These are just a few of the special support considerations that may have to be dealt with.

9
Preparing the Winning Cost Volume

- Top down versus bottom up estimating — what are they? When do you use them?
- How to maximize your profit percentage.
- Some tested pricing strategies.
- Work breakdown structure — the key element for cost control.

The cost proposal applies prices and cost backup to the products or services proposed. Average cost pricing is endorsed by the government and consists of defining the contractor's costs and then adding a reasonable profit. Contractor's costs are verified by government audit.

The procedure for developing overall costs is to have each functional department (engineering, manufacturing, test, training, etc.) submit person-hour and material estimates to an administrator who performs the cost-proposal leader function. Large aerospace companies may have 25 or more departments providing their inputs to a single estimate.

These estimates are made based on a description of the task by the proposal manager and other experts from the proposal team. The accuracy of the resultant estimates will hinge largely on this presentation and the confidence exuded by these technical experts. The pricing department then adds profit to the estimated costs, and management may increase or decrease the final figure (by means of localized or across the board "adjustments") in order to achieve what is believed to be the winning price.

Government agencies typically require the following information in a cost proposal.

- A contract pricing sheet (government form no. DD 633) which is a top-level document for providing certified cost estimates.
- Spread sheets which include breakdowns in column format of the dollar values allocated to person-hours, materials, travel and subsistence, and overhead.

- Lists of materials, equipment, and supplies, the basis of cost estimates (vendor quotations, catalog price sheets, etc.), and the total cost of each item.
- Travel and subsistence forms which explain the purpose, duration, and cost of travel necessary to produce the product or service.
- Narratives which describe the type of labor proposed. These descriptions are task-related and, when possible, compare the effort to past performance.
- Certification of overhead which defines factors used to compute overhead percentages.

Commercial customers may require only material lists, travel and subsistence, and labor breakdowns for their evaluations. On the other hand, some cost proposals consist of nothing more than a price without any further elaboration.

Cost estimation models are usually of two types: top-down and bottom-up. In top-down modeling, the total cost is first derived and then appropriate percentages are allocated to each part of the total task. The allocation may be according to phases, activities, or component parts. Each part can then be further divided into subparts with these costs also allocated in a top-down fashion. In bottom-up modeling, the project is decomposed top-down as before, but costing is not applied until the total subset of pieces is of "manageable size." Costing these pieces is easiest whenever analogous experience with similar completed small pieces can be found. Once the pieces are costed, the total cost is then derived in a bottom-up fashion. Top-down estimation is by far the easier because it is simpler to allocate costs via percentages than via absolutes. Unfortunately, top-down estimation does not reveal how the original total cost is to be derived, and this number is generally the most difficult to determine reliably. Bottom-up estimation is more difficult because the process of independently costing each piece resulting from the decomposition requires more ability, confidence, and effort in detailing design considerations. However, more confidence on the part of the evaluator can be placed in the results of bottom-up estimation. In practice, there is a use for both techniques. Top-down estimation is used for quick, "seat-of-the-pants" budgetaries in preliminary planning, while bottom-up estimation is usually used for formal cost preparation.

Most large companies use some form of task sheet on which the individual departments prepare their work estimates, often with month-by-month labor breakdowns. These are then inputted to a computer where all estimates are added together in like labor categories during like time intervals. The output from the computer process is a summary of costs that may look something like Figure 9.1. Backup sheets would show additional detailed breakdowns in every labor category and distributed over the contract time period month-by-month. Those who use computerized costing are the envy of those who still do the job manually.

The computer is used, of course, to perform many additional costing functions as well. Given overall labor estimates or apportionments, it can automatically provide monthly person-loading and show peaks and valleys of labor demand. It can rapidly calculate absolute costs for a changed contract start date using different then-year dollar values. And it can quickly redo the entire cost estimate when management says "cut everything by 8.375 percent."

A COST REDUCTION STRATEGY

Look for opportunities to reduce your costs by strategic assignment of personnel. An installation team which can provide the dual function of maintenance training is one often-used strategy. This is not a recommendation to charge the government twice for the services of one group of people. Instead, the efficient and above-board use of the same personnel to do both installation and maintenance training tasks can reduce your costs relative to your competitors'.

Accurate cost estimates can often be attributed to accurate and detailed record keeping on previous contracts. A common and serious problem among aerospace and electronics industry contractors is the confusing of accounts for several jobs, making accurate comparisons and extrapolations impossible. Good records, on the other hand, can help to provide a solid base for estimating future jobs.

Under most government contracts, the government requires detailed information on the contractor's costs. The contractor must certify

	TYPICAL FACTOR (% OF TOTAL COST)	PERSON-HRS	DOLLARS
PROGRAM OFFICE COSTS			
Program Manager			
Administrative Assistant			
Secretary			
NONRECURRING COSTS			
Hardware Design Engineering			
Software Design Engineering			
Tradeoff Studies			
Prototyping/Breadboarding			
Computer Time/Electronic Data Processing			
Consultants			
Travel and Subsistence			
Tooling			
Drawings			
Test Equipment			
Operation & Maintenance Manual			
Test Procedures			
Technical Report			
RECURRING COSTS			
Materials			
Procurement			
Manufacturing			
Assembly			
Quality Control Inspections			
Spares			
Packing & Shipping			
Installation			
Test			
Expendables (magnetic tape, photographic film, fuel, etc.)			
OTHER COSTS			
Bid & Proposal			
Independent Research & Development Overhead			
General & Administrative Expense			
Facilities			
Security			
Warranty			
TOTAL COST			
FEE AND PROFIT			
COST OF MONEY/INTEREST EXPENSE			

Fig. 9.1 Checklist of cost proposal content.

that the cost data submitted is accurate, current, and complete. The price may be adjusted downward if it is found through audit procedure that the data were not as certified. Figure 9.2 gives a few strategy suggestions regarding cost estimating and price determination.

SYSTEM CONFIGURATION

The system engineer, assisted by the engineering department, should define the system configuration during the early part of the proposal effort. The system configuration, to an assembly level, should be defined on subsystem breakdown sheets. Entries for each assembly should be defined on subsystem breakdown sheets. Entries for each assembly should detail the requirements of:

- Operational departments for allocating hours and material dollars to specific tasks, and
- Specific and general bid costs.

- Provide a cost summary which includes a cost breakdown of both labor and materials.
- Explain your estimating procedures and the basis of your estimates.
- State your terms and conditions.
- In procurements in which a "best and final offer" is solicited, make the initial cost submittal in anticipation of changing it downward or upward or, sometimes, not changing it at all for that final submittal.
- In design-to-cost procurements, prototype cost (nonrecurring + recurring) should not exceed 2 1/2 times the recurring cost objective.
- If you're Numero Uno technically, your price shouldn't be more than 10 percent above No. 2 technically. Conversely, if you're not No. 1 technically, you'd better have a price *more than* 10 percent below the technical leader.
- Don't blindly lower your price when "best and final offer" (BAFO) is asked for.
- On large programs find out the budget approved by Congress. Rarely will this be the actual amount of the awarded contract, but it's a rough guide and serves as a starting point in determining the price you should shoot for.
- Readily identifiable physical milestones should be proposed to facilitate progress payments.
- Don't forget to consider the effects of "then dollars" versus "now dollars" in your estimates. (The larger future dollar amounts are sometimes euphemistically called "performing-year" dollars.)
- Remember that costs of production generally drop somewhere between 15 and 30 percent for every doubling of production.
- Finally, when an individual item can only be produced at a financial loss, it is very difficult to make it up on volume.

Fig. 9.2 Cost volume strategies.

DESIGN REVIEW

Each functional department should send representatives to the design reviews held periodically during the proposal's preparation. Questions should be resolved at these meetings so that all departments have the same understanding of the task.

WORK BREAKDOWN STRUCTURE

The work breakdown structure (WBS) offers an effective systems approach to the makeup of any cost proposal. A WBS breaks the program, product, or service into smaller, more manageable parts which can be individually costed. The total program is established as the first level of the WBS. Levels 2, 3, etc., are successively lower levels of the program or product. When only the upper three levels are presented, the WBS is referred to as a summary work breakdown structure.

One way to structure a WBS is to make a family tree arrangement according to function, where the individual WBS elements are operations to be carried out. Figure 9.3 illustrates this kind of organization and represents the software system for a flight simulator. Each

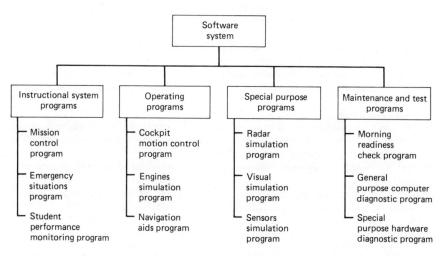

Fig. 9.3 Top level work breakdown structure exhibit, illustrating the software system for a flight simulator.

program of this example would typically consist of several software modules which themselves could be illustrated by another WBS like Figure 9.4, for example. A WBS might also be organized according to physical boundaries, showing items and subsystems of hardware. Or it might simply be organized to reflect the RFP/SOW structure.

Proposal writers should recognize that a good WBS is well organized and gives a complete top-to-bottom, general-to-specific breakdown of the product. Accordingly, the WBS can constitute an excellent basis for a logical and complete proposal outline showing each author how his input fits into the total effort and where each WBS element constitutes one subtopic within the outline. If you've got a good WBS, don't overlook this effective outlining strategy.

WORK PACKAGES

Once the product or service has been logically and systematically subdivided into its component parts by a WBS, the work required to produce each of these parts can be estimated. These smaller, more manageable estimates are called work packages and their form varies among different companies, but their content generally includes the following.

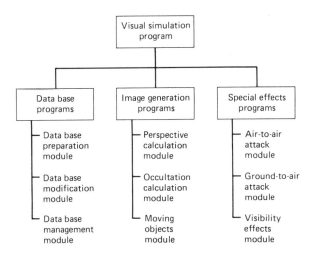

Fig. 9.4 Work breakdown structure exhibit, illustrating the next finer level of software system detail.

- What is the task to be accomplished?
- By whom?
- What resources are required?
- Within what time schedule must the task be completed?

The work package, therefore, defines a specific task and provides a basis for measuring work progress and for determining when work is to be completed.

The WBS and work packages show the elements of work which make up the total program but do not show task sequences interconnected to form an overall program schedule. The next logical step then, is to develop a network diagram of the work packages with detailed time estimates included for each work package segment of the network. One kind of network is known as a Program Evaluation and Review Technique (PERT) diagram, and makes the elapsed time necessary to complete the total program and any portion of the program highly visible. The level of detail in the WBS, the work packages, and the PERT diagram can be made high or low depending upon the extent of management planning and control visibility that is needed or wanted.

Upon contract award, the work packages that were assembled while estimating the program costs will become work authorizations to help control the performance of the actual tasks. If they have been correctly put together, they will indicate what work is to be done, who shall perform the work, what resources are needed, and within what time schedule the work is to be completed.

In making the transition from a proposal stage work package to a contract stage work authorization, the packages should be updated to reflect any changes in the requirements which take place during contract negotiations.

COST INPUTS FROM FUNCTIONAL DEPARTMENTS

The functional departments should prepare bid packages which include person-loadings, work statements, cost narratives to backup labor estimates, material breakdowns, and an internal memorandum calling the attention of management to risk and problem areas. The cost proposal leader should compile this data and prepare a number of charts to:

- Outline the ground rules and assumptions used in developing the costs.
- Show the cost of the effort in person-hours and dollars by major department.
- Specify the risk areas and the level of the risk.
- Specify major buy items.
- Show confidence level for all estimates.
- Show how other programs, on-going, past experience, or anticipated new business have influenced the estimates.
- Recommend a bid price and give justification for the recommendation.

Many costing efforts waste hundreds, even thousands of person-hours because too little time is spent explaining the overall task and establishing reasonable limits for the many sub-tasks. When operating in an environment of too little information, estimators will tend to "play it safe" and estimate many more hours and include unnecessary contingencies. Such profligate estimates will sometimes exceed the customer's budget for the program by several orders of magnitude, and the end result is that the whole thing has to be done over again.

An effective way to combat gross overestimates is to first ask for a rough cut estimate, without detailed backup and without month-by-month person-loading. All that is asked for initially is an approximation perhaps to the nearest person-year that each functional manager believes the program will require. Then, call the group together, tabulate the results for everyone's perusal, and point out and discuss areas which are unreasonably high or low. Using known overhead rates, the total labor hours can be quickly converted to dollars, add rough material costs, add administrative costs and profit, and then compare the bottom line number with what is believed to be the customer's budget. But do all this *before* entering into a detailed cost estimate. It's amazing how many contractors don't.

REVIEW BY THE PROPOSAL MANAGER

Usually, it is up to the proposal program manager to analyze the cost data from the departments and negotiate lower or higher estimates if their cost projections seem unreasonable.

The proposal manager and the cost proposal leader should review the inputs from functional departments, comparing past performance and bids on similar systems. The proposal manager should meet with people from functional departments to resolve problem areas. A basis for most bids will be a detailed bottom-up analysis. That is, a bill of material is prepared subsystem by subsystem until the total system configuration is accounted for. Where such detail isn't required, the estimating basis may be less rigorous and estimates may be made by making comparisons to existing equipment or may be simply based upon expert opinion. However accomplished, estimates should be compiled and entered on cost summary pages, sometimes called spread sheets.

ENGINEERING REVIEW

Each department manager should review and approve the spread sheets. He should compose a bid ground-rules letter to state assumptions, additions, and deletions relative to similar company products, as well as exceptions, and any other information affecting the bid.

PRICING

Material and labor costs plus overhead and other expenses, plus profit all equal price. The finance department should price the bid according to predicted wage rates, overhead, and profit factors. A price confirmation sheet, approved by the finance manager, should be attached to the priced spread sheet in preparation for the final "bid meeting" or review by top management.

Profit is the return to the owners for assuming the risks of development or production. The margin of profit that the government will allow is not determined arbitrarily. Instead, contractors are asked to justify the profit objective, using a system of weighted guidelines. The weighted guidelines method combines various criteria to yield a profit percentage based largely on earlier contractor performance. The weighted summation process is illustrated in Figure 9.5.

Past contractor performance in areas of contractor effort, contractor risks, facilities investment, and other special factors are combined arithmetically in an attempt to increase the contractor's claimed profit

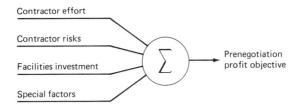

Fig. 9.5 The weighted summation technique for determining the prenegotiation profit objective.

objective. A new program that is on the edge of the art, for example, can cause more problems and require more managerial time and abilities of a high order. It may require scarce or unusual engineering talent. And it may require management of subcontracting programs involving many sources and detailed and complex purchase specifications. These can be justifications for a higher profit percentage than a follow-on contract, for example.

The procurement contracting officer may request that contractors develop their profit objective based on these or some other criteria. DD Form 1547 provides detailed guidance on using the weighted guidelines technique.

TOP MANAGEMENT REVIEW

The final bid meeting should be arranged by the proposal manager. Typically, the general manager, proposal manager, representatives of the product line, marketing, engineering, finance, and contracts departments are invited to attend. Technical risk, schedule risk, and financial risk should be thoroughly discussed and the results documented. The marketing representative should provide a competitive evaluation as well as a recommended selling price. A transmittal letter, often called the "cover letter," is usually prepared by marketing, and should be reviewed by those in attendance. Upon approval, the cover letter and spread sheets should be signed by the general manager.

10
The Critical Red Team Process
for Proposal Review

- The Who, What, Why, When, Where, and How of the red team process.
- Proposal improvements that you can expect from the red team process.
- Some problems that the red team won't solve.

When the sought after contract is crucial to your company's continued existence, it's time to pull out all the stops and strive for the ultimate in proposal perfection. An effective finalization procedure for detecting and correcting your proposal faults is to form a "red team" which, in essence, performs an internal evaluation of your proposal and imitates your customer's evaluation team. Like the proposal team, the successful red team relies on talented people banding together for a short time. It's expensive, and will use up a lot of your discretionary resources in a hurry, but if you're competing for a giant procurement you can't afford to not use the red team process.

Red team members should *imitate* their counterparts on the customer's evaluation team. They should work independently and produce independent scoring and marked-up drafts (not rewrites). Figures 10.1 and 10.2 illustrate sample forms and rating systems that can be used to score a proposal. Figure 10.1 is designed for rating technical volumes, whereas Figure 10.2 can have more general application including management and administrative material. As Figures 10.1 and 10.2 illustrate, red team criticisms should be specific, not wishy-washy generalizations.

During the early stages of the proposal effort, the red team should train for their assignment by studying the RFP and, in particular, by

Program _____ Volume _____ Section _____ Evaluation and grading	Excellent/ superior	Satisfactory	Weak	Unacceptable
General criteria	(8-10)	(5-7)	(3-4)	(0-2)
• Soundness and adequacy of design to meet performance requirements.				
• Soundness of approach in minimizing cost and technical risk.				
• Effective use of low risk design techniques.				
• Ingenuity and imagination of design concept.				
• Evidence of low cost approach.				
• Quality of response (readability/understanding, logical presentation/approach, ease of evaluation, correlation to RFP/ SOW/specs, believability, etc.)				

Comments/recomendations

Fig. 10.1 Grading sheet suitable for scoring of a technical volume by a red team.

becoming intimately familiar with the criteria for evaluation. That is, what will the technical evaluators actually do, feel, and look for?

MAKEUP OF THE RED TEAM

Ideally, and aside from technical expertise, the red team should consist of people with the ability to commit themselves quickly to a short project, have the temperament to call a spade a spade and say exactly what they think, and be able to tolerate the stress of an extremely short schedule.

The team can consist of one to fifteen or so people; they should be from the ranks of middle management and the senior scientific and engineering staff. Outside consultants are ideally suited to what the red team must do. None should be from the proposal team itself and none should be from upper levels of management. A vice president, for example, is probably the worst candidate for a red team. He won't read or

PROGRAM _____

VOLUME _____

SECTION _____   EVALUATION

CRITERIA	GOOD	AVERAGE	INADE-QUATE	NOT APPLIC-ABLE	CANNOT JUDGE
1. READABILITY?	☐	☐	☐	☐	☐
2. LOGICALLY DEVELOPED ARGUMENT?	☐	☐	☐	☐	☐
3. PERSUASIVENESS?	☐	☐	☐	☐	☐
4. COMPLIANT?	☐	☐	☐	☐	☐
5. IS THE PROPOSAL AN ATTRACTIVE SALES PACKAGE?	☐	☐	☐	☐	☐

SPECIFIC COMMENTS: _____.

_____

_____

_____

_____

_____

_____

_____

_____

_____

SPECIFIC SUGGESTIONS: _____

_____

_____

_____

_____

_____

_____

_____

Fig. 10.2 Grading sheet suitable for scoring of management and logistics support volumes by a red team.

have time to read the RFP and its specifications, and he will invariably base his critique on intuition rather than on customer requirements. In difficult times, hunches just aren't good enough. Intuitive judgements from the uninformed are wrong much of the time, and wrong judgements aren't what is needed when a large investment is at stake.

Figure 10.3 provides a summary checklist for red team makeup and review of a proposal.

RED TEAM PROCEDURES

Team members should read the entire proposal and score each major section based on the evaluation criteria. The scores are no help to the proposal team as far as telling them what needs to be done, but they identify the sections needing the most work. *The real value in what the red team does is in the specific criticisms that each reviewer should note in the draft copies of the proposal.* Time is getting short, so the more specific the comment the better its chances are of being taken care of. Vague criticisms like "this doesn't grab me" aren't much use and won't be appreciated by a tired author or proposal editor.

Comments in the review copies should be merged, and this can be an extremely challenging editorial task when there are ten or so red team reviewers. Many will criticize the same items, in doing so their recommendations can range from being the same, to a shade different, and all the way to being oppositely polarized. The editor who does the merger needs impeccable judgement as well as complete and detailed understanding of the problem.

- Pick red team members based upon competence, proposal subject knowledge and outspokenness.
- Review proposal from a customer standpoint.
- Use the same criteria the customer source selection committee will use:
  - Evaluation criteria & factors.
  - Responsiveness to RFP.
- Prepare rating sheets for each criteria and proposal section identifying:
  - Deficiencies.
  - Weak points.
  - Recommendations for improvement.
  - Grading of response.

Fig. 10.3 Checklist for red team review of the proposal.

TYPICAL RED TEAM RESULTS

Long ago I became a believer in the proposal philosophy, "Tell them what you're going to tell them, tell them, and then tell them what you told them." The most common proposal fault that I've seen as a red team reviewer is that authors only present the "tell them" or the middle part of the above expression. That is, there is seldom an adequate introduction to a technical section and rarely is there a wrap-up or "Tell them what you told them" paragraph at all. There is only a middle."

So as a reviewer, I find myself most frequently being critical of missing or inadequate baseline introductions, as well as mid-air endings that beg for a summary. These and other reasons why costly bidding efforts so often fail are listed in Figure 10.4.

A sometimes-heard criticism of the red team process is that despite the theoretical desirability of the approach, it is impractical for the red team to faithfully imitate the customer's reactions to the proposal. This is because the team will not be exposed to the real intricacies of the problem or to the months of pre-selling activity on the part of all the potential contractors. Two days of RFP review may be their only indoctrination. The red team, in fact, will not likely know the customer at all. But despite those drawbacks, the red team process has been shown to result in extremely worthwhile improvements to a proposal.

- Doesn't state benefits to the user.
- Doesn't state advantages relative to competition.
- Lacks innovative approach.
- Not responsive to RFP and/or correlates poorly with RFP.
- Begins with detail and ends with detail; i.e., the proposal has no theme, executive-level summary or overview.
- Vagueness of intent; superficial and noncommital treatment; lacking in clarity and in-depth analysis; foggy prose.
- Unsupported statements and conclusions.
- Factual inaccuracies, distortion, gaping holes.
- Not persuasively written.
- Shallow treatment of high risk areas.
- Improperly assumes customer has prior knowledge of the company, its capabilities, and its experience. Thus, fails to display the true resources of the company.
- Goldplating; i.e., proposes features beyond minimum requirements.
- Platitudinous writing; turgid, stilted, or ambiguous prose.
- Slipshod appearance.
- Poor grammar and sentence structure, bad spelling and general confusion.
- Too wordy; mountainous prose with mouse-size meaning.
- Not compliant.
- Not logical.
- Discontinuous.
- Missing or buried conclusions.
- Nonadherence to proposal preparation instructions.
- Proposal poorly conceived and poorly executed.
- Poor selection of project manager and/or key personnel.
- Poorly conceived man/machine relationships and interfaces.
- Obsolete management, design, and/or testing practices.
- Lack of resources to do the work.
- Started from scratch at RFP release; inadequate time and resources to do a proper job in preparing the proposal.

Fig. 10.4 The most common proposal faults.

11
Putting It All Together

- The editor and the editing process.
- Qualifications of a technical proposal editor.
- What does a good editor do?
- Group editing.
- Nice finishing touches.
- The revision collection cycle — what is it? What can it do for you?
- How to stay within page limits.
- Production tips.
- How to write the cover letter.
- Delivery

Good writing is, of course, a main ingredient of a winning proposal. A common cause of poor proposals is the need to coordinate the writings of different groups within the company. On one side, there is the danger that contradictory statements will slip through because not enough editing was done. This raises the suspicion that your proposal team doesn't know what it is doing. The other danger, in an effort to avoid contradictions or major omissions, is that the proposal becomes too rigid and so is unreadable and stilted. There is a fine line between these two extremes.

Proposals and, in fact, all documents that go outside a company should be channeled through skilled writer/editors so that consistent standards of style, format, and company policy are met and presented to the outside world. Skillful editing can also ensure that the material doesn't compromise existing contractual agreements, disturb customer relations, or reveal classified or proprietary information. Contradictions and inconsistencies in proposals can be especially damaging to your chances of winning. But editing is frequently the most hectic part of producing a proposal because too often the outlines and schedule are treated with a cavalier attitude or are even ignored by others in the proposal preparation process. Ninety percent of the work, including all of the editing, then becomes jammed into the last ten percent of the time available.

THE TECHNICAL PROPOSAL EDITOR AND
HIS QUALIFICATIONS

A good proposal editor should be an effective communicator, with technical training, a marketing orientation, and strong writing and editing skills. He or she should be able to research, analyze, and summarize technical information for technical and executive readers. And to support preproposal, proposal, and postproposal phases, the editor should be able to plan, organize, and carry out many different kinds of communications projects efficiently.

A technical proposal editor does not have to be a specialist in depth in all fields. But he should know what is reasonable to do in the various fields in which he will be called upon to edit, and sometimes originate, material. His is an important job, for in a very real sense he determines what goes into the proposal and what doesn't.

The editor shouldn't be too specialized — too narrow in his outlook — he needs breadth. He needs to know general principles and should have basic knowledge of lots of things. He doesn't have to know how to design a computer, radar system, or TV, but if these are his company's products, he should have a pretty good understanding of what is possible. He can then be objective in his editing and writing, knowing what to highlight and by how much, and he can also spot distortions and outright errors by others.

The background of a good technical editor will touch upon many fields of study. His formal education might include a journalism or English degree, but he should have training or at least a strong interest in engineering and science. He should have superior writing ability and should feel at home with the rules of grammar. For postproposal presentations, he should also have skills in multimedia preparation, including printing, audio-visual, film and video tape techniques, and be able to communicate well with multidisciplinary engineering personnel. His duties are summarized in Figure 11.1.

- Edit, write, and rewrite proposal inputs.
- Compare proposal inputs against customer specification and other proposal sections to ensure technical correctness, compatibility, and lack of contradiction.
- Check sentences, paragraphs, and sections for clarity and conciseness.
- Assist in preparing presentation materials and advertising literature. This will include agendas, flipcharts, viewgraphs, and other marketing aids.
- Compose and update employee resumes.
- Compose and update related experience descriptions.
- Compose and update facilities descriptions.
- Perform general editing and rewrite services.

Fig. 11.1 Checklist of proposal editor duties.

But perhaps the most useful trait of a good proposal editor is the ability to transform his mental attitudes to those of the proposal evaluator, complete with his likes, dislikes, education, and experience background. If this mental transformation can be accomplished at will, while the proposal is being written, then skillful editing and shaping of the proposal can be achieved.

WHAT DOES A GOOD EDITOR DO?

"I'm sorry I've written such a long letter; if I'd had more time, I'd have written you a shorter one." The anonymous author of this seemingly contradictory sentence knows what editing is all about.

WHAT DOES A GOOD EDITOR DO?

A savvy technical editor will routinely do certain basic things to every proposal manuscript. Usually, these routine tasks will include generating "active" titles and subheads, rewriting section openings to increase reader interest, and preparing descriptive captions for illustrations. Many of the techniques that an editor may elect to apply are listed in Figure 11.2.

The editor may sometimes have to perform major surgery such as subordinating facts and concepts into a disciplined order with proper relative emphasis — neither attaching undue significance to minor points nor burying major points. He should know how to make a long dissertation short, a fuzzy description crisp. He should know how to

- Use the fewest number of words consistent with clarity.
- Use the least complex word available. Use the most specific word; use exact word when available.
- Tighten each sentence – avoid repeated use of conjunctions such as *and* and *or.*
- Order sentences according to the best sequence for understanding; subordinate thoughts.
- Consider the recipient (audience). What do you know about him? Approach proposal with a "you attitude" as opposed to merely displaying the knowledge of the writer.
- Use the active voice instead of the passive voice particularly when the active verbs don't require personal pronouns as subjects. Active verb forms, in general, tend to be clearer and more interesting to read.
- Personify the inanimate. Instead of saying "the operating procedure is described in the manual," say "the manual describes the operating procedure." Even though the manual is seemingly given a human attribute, the clarity and conciseness of the statement is improved.
- Tastefully informalize some of your writing by use of contractions, personal pronouns, similes, and even a bit of slang.
- Avoid run-on sentences. Check all sentences over 20 to 25 words long for possible division into two sentences.
- Intersperse short sentences with long ones. Use one-sentence paragraphs occasionally; it's no sin.
- Add tasteful testimonial such as "Dr. _____, our Director of Advanced Programs, stated that this proposed investigation can save a million dollars in production costs."
- Be persuasive. Show a tasteful amount of eagerness and enthusiasm without resorting to blatant advertising.
- Be specific; eliminate generalities.
- Edit ruthlessly. Words are like inflated dollars – the more you use, the less each one is worth. Go through your entire proposal as many times as it takes. Remove all the deadwood: unnecessary words, sentences – even paragraphs.

Fig. 11.2 Strategies for good writing.

explain complicated, high-risk processes so adroitly that the proposal evaluator will never realize that he is in a minefield. He should pay attention to paragraph opening words and phrases, with an eye toward stimulating reader interest. Connectives like those in Figure 11.3 make the narrative flow instead of appearing as a listing of disjointed topics. An editor faced with a write-up consisting of all short sentences, for example, should join a few of them with *and, but, because, or,* and the connectives listed in Figure 11.3. In any event, the editor should make sure that every paragraph doesn't start with "The." Finally, he makes his mark by asking the hard questions: Is it logical? Is it persuasive? Is it compliant?

Like a good news story reporter, the technical editor should not be satisfied until he has asked himself many questions pertaining to principles of good writing. Every editor has his own mentally applied tests to determine whether the written material should be changed.

RELATIONSHIP TO BE DENOTED	SUGGESTED TRANSITION WORD OR PHASE
Example	Consider Now let us consider . . . Consider for discussion . . . To illustrate . . . One might also consider . . . For instance . . . To see this more clearly, consider . . . What follows is our best estimate of . . . For example . . .
Additional Supporting Argument	To understand why . . . Moreover . . . Furthermore . . . Similarly . . . Equally important . . . Next in importance . . . In like manner . . . Additional insight into . . . It is well known that . . . If one asks . . . the answer is . . . Less well known is . . . Growing evidence points to . . . A growing number of experts are beginning to . . . To go beyond generalizations . . . The crucial factor is . . . This perhaps is obvious, but what may not be so obvious is . . . To dig more deeply . . . In the same vein . . .
Counterargument	Conversely . . . On the other hand . . . In contrast . . . The previous discussion dealt with . . . While some observers question . . . In spite of the conventional wisdom that says . . .
Emphasis and restatement	Now a very significant point . . . Simply put . . . In other words . . . Never before has . . . What lifts this approach above the ordinary is . . . Designers failing to perceive the need for . . . The central concept in this development is . . . Success in this development lies in . . . Broadly speaking . . . In our view . . .
Conclusion	All of which brings us to . . . Recall that we said . . . In summary . . . In conclusion . . . The conclusion is reached that . . . All in all . . . Not surprisingly . . . In short . . . As you might expect . . .

Fig. 11.3 Connectives that can help make your narratives flow.

Here are a few questions which may help you stimulate your own editing techniques.

Relocate? Would the main points of the technical write-up have greater impact if positioned somewhere else?
Eliminate? Is the word, phrase, sentence, or paragraph critical to convey proper meaning or to avoid misunderstanding? Suppose it wasn't there at all?
Shorten? Is the write-up too long? Too complicated? Too detailed?
Lengthen? Have all important aspects been discussed? Have all the questions *Who? Why? What? Where? When?* and *How?* been answered?
Simplify? Does the write-up use active rather than passive voice? Does it use the most exact words throughout? Is it easy to read — short paragraphs, frequent headings, section dividers, standard abbreviations?
Accelerate? Does the write-up get to the main point quickly or is it obtuse and roundabout?
Transpose? Should certain points be interchanged to achieve greater emphasis or clarity?
Change Emphasis? Does the write-up give too much attention to minor things, not enough attention to major things?
Reorder? Does the write-up use primacy- or recency-based ordering, for example?

A common mistake made by engineer-authors is to define acronyms and then not use them, or to use them randomly, or to define acronyms which simply aren't needed. If the acronym never gets used after it's defined, it wasn't needed in the first place. Good technical editors will spot these kinds of errors right off. A common language glossary of terms and abbreviations handed out at the kickoff meeting is a far more painless way to achieve consistent terminology and avoid errors in usage of acronyms. (See Appendix A for a list of common acronyms encountered in many RFP's.)

Finally, the thorough technical editor will create and include in every proposal a cross-index that references sections of the customer specification, statement of work, and technical proposal requirements documents to sections of the proposal. Inclusion of a cross-index helps give the evaluators a "warm feeling" that all the requirements have

USE CONSISTENT TERMINOLOGY

Too little attention is sometimes paid to the terms we use in proposals, particularly in regard to their consistency from sentence to sentence, paragraph to paragraph, and section to section. Unless you've been an evaluator or a member of a red team, you may not fully appreciate how disheartening it can be to encounter half a dozen terms, all meaning the same thing. One recent proposal for a multimillion dollar simulator had all of the following labels applied to one portion of the system configuration:

Computational system   Control computer
Computational subsystem   Control computer subsystem
Computer system   Control computer complex
Computer subsystem   Computer complex

All were used interchangeably in the final draft, and close inspection by the technical editor revealed that all referred to exactly the same thing – a commercial minicomputer with three peripherals. This may not always be the case. "Computer" may sometimes be used to designate only the central processing unit, whereas "computer subsystem" could designate all computer hardware and software. If these kind of subtle distinctions are important, say so. But don't use different words and phrases to designate the same thing. Evaluators can get very upset when they're left to wonder whether different terms are used to convey an important distinction.

been addressed without actually having to go through a laborious item-by-item check of a proposal. An example of a cross-index, relating only technical specification paragraphs to proposal paragraphs, is shown in Figure 11.4. Note that the customer's document is the independent variable (indexed in numerical sequence) in any such cross-reference. The idea, of course, is to make *his* job easier in locating particular sections-of-interest.

We have barely touched upon elements of good editing. Any greater depth is perhaps better left to specialists and the many books that exhaustively treat virtually all aspects of good writing. (A representative

RFP TECHNICAL SPECIFICATION	OUR PROPOSAL
1.0 Installation	6.0
1.1 Space Requirements	6.1, 6.2
1.2 Power Requirements	6.3
1.3 Test Equipment and Tool Requirements	5.3
2.0 General System Description	3.0,3.3,3.4
2.1 Operating Principles	3.2
2.2 Operating Specifications	3.1
3.0 Operating Procedures	3.5
3.1 System Turn-On	3.5.1
3.2 Film Loading	3.5.2
3.3 Alignment and Calibration	5.4
3.4 Film Reading	3.2
3.5 System Turn-Off	3.5.3
4.0 Maintenance	5.2
4.1 Preventive Maintenance	5.2.1
4.2 Troubleshooting	5.2.2

Fig. 11.4 A cross-reference index shows the evaluator where his specification is addressed.

few are listed in Appendix E.) Remember though that editing, like writing, is something that can't be done well unless one keeps in practice.

NEW CONCEPTS IN PROPOSAL EDITING

Traditional methods of proposal editing and production are giving way to computer-managed word processing systems that perform the same tasks. The advent of the digital computer has revolutionized past concepts of editing and word processing by out-performing past methods in speed, accuracy, and completeness of detail. Devices and systems have extended the application of computers from accounting to text editing and data base storage, management, and retrieval. Input/output is provided by automated typewriters and interactive cathode-ray tube terminals with keyboard control and high-speed printer output, often with typeset quality suitable for direct use as the printing masters. Some have added optical character recognition (OCR) as a means for entering text to the system. These are all generally referred to as word processing systems.

Word processing systems can dramatically reduce the time needed to produce proposals and, at the same time, can improve their appearance. When edited drafts are retyped, for example, only the new or changed material needs to be keyboarded and typographical mistakes become fewer with each draft. Unchanged text is reproduced error-free from the machine memory — usually floppy disk, magnetic cards, or magnetic tape. Retyping time is thereby reduced as is proofreading time since typographic errors are fewer.

Editors who edit on TV-like display terminals instead of paper will soon be the envy of anyone who continues to process text using traditional methods. Computer-aided text processing systems are becoming less expensive and purchase will soon extend beyond large aerospace companies, falling within the price reach of smaller and smaller industrial users.

In the more advanced word processing systems, there is already no need for editors to learn how to structure commands in computer syntax. They can revise author manuscripts just by tapping out memo-like instructions using conversational English notation.

On the edge-of-the-art is proposal preparation using sophisticated data base management system software coupled with word-processing software and hardware. Standard paragraphs are retrieved based on key words and phrases and a file search algorithm. These paragraphs are examined on a CRT screen and are "customized." Customizing can consist of substituting a different customer name, system name or acronym, and revising performance specifications. The revised text reflecting the current proposal situation is then merged with other text and graphics to provide camera-ready page masters, ready for the printer.

These kind of systems are already in widespread use in the newspaper industry easing the jobs of reporters, editors, typists, and compositors. In terms of editing, organizing, and rewriting, they provide substantial improvements in productivity.

The growing interest in text processing systems stems from their increased productivity and their ability to slash lead time and errors considerably. Far fewer keystrokes are needed in progressing from initial draft through several stages of revision to final, camera-ready copy. Moreover, the ease with which changes are made will encourage editors to do more rework and polishing, resulting in higher quality output.

The real advances in word processing capabilities will take place when graphics handling and text handling can take place intermixed within computer memory. Computers will then be able to assemble camera-ready pages without manual intervention and paste-up processes.

THE GROUP THERAPY METHOD OF EDITING

An editing technique effective in weeding out misconceptions is to read aloud what has been written in silence. A list of recommended listeners should include the technical author(s) and at least two other persons familiar with the subject. One person serves as the senior editor while each writer's material is read aloud and commented upon. A helpful strategy, particularly when the evaluation criteria are known, is to develop your own scoring model and to then rate each section of the proposal objectively after reading it aloud. Group therapy is expensive in terms of person-hours, but it can be very effective.

> *GROUP EDITING IN PRACTICE*
>
> *The group edit will usually correct any faults which are in the draft but things which have been overlooked tend to remain overlooked. That is, the group edit is not effective in correcting errors of omission. In my own experience, I have found that the momentum of the group edit seems to discourage much reflection upon things that might be missing. Another risk is that by trying to please everyone in the group, all controversial material gets eliminated and the proposal becomes bland. However, a strong senior editor can guard against this.*

THE REVISION COLLECTION CYCLE

Proposal work is severely limited by time, and there is usually no room for false starts or extensive rework. However, when there is some breathing room in the schedule, quantum improvements can be made in the text by a feedback mechanism referred to as the revision collection cycle. Simply put, the revision collection cycle consists of distributing preprints called revision collection copies (RCC's) of the total proposal among the proposal team and other reviewers. Then, everyone's comments and recommendations are merged by an editor. In effect, the eyes of many editors are brought to bear on the proposal draft, and with fast reproduction and distribution, the RCC strategy can significantly shorten the editing cycle. The revision collection cycle is represented by the dotted feedback path on the proposal preparation plan shown in Figure 1.6b and 1.6c (see pages 11-12); it allows a complete recycle through design, review, editing, and rewriting phases of the technical proposal preparation process. Every contributor, therefore, is afforded the opportunity to see his input in relation to the whole and to make modifications where appropriate. As many as five revision collection cycles have been effectively applied by this author to a single proposal.

If you have trouble getting timely responses to the RCC's, try an insidious little memo saying, "The latest date for review comments on the _____ proposal is September 24. If we haven't received any comments by that date, we will assume the draft is perfect *and has been approved by you.*"

NICE FINISHING TOUCHES

The intent of this book is to help the average proposal writer lift the average proposal above this averageness and to make it something special. If you've followed many of the strategies and recommendations presented so far, much of what is needed to accomplish this has already been done. It remains but to add a touch of elegance, making the proposal look as good as it sounds. Figure 11.5 lists a few tips and recommendations which can result in a high-order improvement.

Modern techniques should be used throughout the proposal. For example, wherever the need for punctuation, hyphenation in particular, is optional, suppress it.

Wherever a word has alternate spellings (*focus* vs. *focuss, accomodate* vs. *accommodate, judgment* vs. *judgement, skilfully* vs. *skillfully, programing* vs. *programming,* etc.), use the most efficient form, i.e., the version requiring the fewest keystrokes except for cases in which popular usage dictates otherwise. The object is not to save keystrokes, but to achieve spelling consistency. If the alternate spellings have no efficiency advantage, adopt one version as your standard and stick to it. *Disk* versus *disc* is a case in point. Some proposal writers, including this author, feel that *disk* should be used for computer-related storage devices, one reason being consistency with its derivative *diskette.* Others feel that "disc" should be used.

Wherever states are designated, use the standard two-letter capitalized abbreviations with all punctuation eliminated (see Appendix D).

- Photographically reduce all text by 10 percent. This gives text a printed quality as opposed to a typed quality. Emphasize key points with bold, manually-inked underlines – no typewriter underlines. Alternatively, use capitalization or contrasting type styles to emphasize strategic or critical issues.
- Minimize "turn pages" . . . pages that necessitate turning the proposal ninety degrees in order to be read.
- Use contrasting color paper to highlight strategic pages.
- Photographically inset the cover letter onto the first page of the technical or management volumes.
- Use magazine-style sidebar (lined off inset) descriptions to amplify key issues. Make these sidebars stand out by using bold outlines, background tints, and contrasting type style.
- Typeset all paragraph headings; typeset the entire proposal.
- Add descriptive captions (sometimes called "thematic titling") on all visuals so that each stands alone as a textual/visual entity. It should be possible then, to follow the main points of the proposal by reading the captions without necessarily reading the proposal text.
- Use inset paragraphs and/or change type face for emphasis.
- Use heavy stock, tab-type separator pages for easy access to proposal subsections. A brief executive summary of section content printed on the tabular separator adds a touch of class.
- Use multiple colors or gray shade local tinting to clarify complex flow diagrams, electronic system or circuit diagrams, and the like. Don't use color merely for aesthetic reasons.
- Print the proposal on distinctive, pastel-shaded, high quality paper.
- Use double column, justified format for best space utilization, fastest readability, and most attractive appearance.
- Of the two accepted ways of punctuating a series (A,B, and C *or* A,B and C), choose one way and adopt it as your company standard. (Note that A,B, and C is the only version that grants equal status to all three items in the series; A,B and C couples 'B' and 'C' in a special, closer relationship from which 'A' is excluded. Punctuation makes clear the writer's real intention.)
- Include a glossary of acronymns, initialisms, and abbreviations that are used in the proposal. Locate the glossary up front, on the first section divider of each volume, for example.

Fig. 11.5 Strategies for improving the appearance and physical impact of your proposal.

For pagination of the text, number each section sequentially 1-1, 1-2, 1-3 . . . 2-1, 2-2, 2-3. . . . If you number straight through (1,2,3, 4 . . .), you'll have trouble making eleventh hour changes to the proposal.

When capitalization is optional, resist the urge to glorify unimportant terms. The modern trend is to simplify, clarify, and thereby speed reading. Generally, a sentence dotted throughout with capitals slows reading, especially if the words are unambiguous without the caps. Often over time, words that began unequivocally as proper names are lowercased by common consent – *hertz, ohm,* and so on.

Be alert also to modern trends in making compounds (words made up to two or more distinct words, either in solid or hyphenated form) from words which were previously two-word and three-word phrases. Witness *real-time/realtime* (hovering now between hyphenated and closed up), *worldwide, heartbeat, cathode-ray tube, backup, pickup, daytime, fourfold, playoff, fallout, tie-up, take-off, under way, spin-off, close-up, know-how, carry-over*?) Technical words that were originally two include *down-time, voiceprint, time-sharing* (though *time base* is still generally used), *printout, crosstalk, checksum, uplink,* and *downlink.*

Sprinkle the text with brief, editorialized executive summaries. A sidebar is an effective way to summarize as well as add supporting peripheral arguments that may lie just outside the mainstream narrative. Sidebars, or insets as they are often called, are asides which support and flesh out an argument but are not essential to the basic theme. A sidebar on page one of each proposal volume, for example, might list the themes of each respective volume, forcibly introducing these vital messages to the evaluator and providing a handy, quick reference of what follows. The sidebar isn't essential to the volume's content, but it can aid the speed and ease with which the reader can absorb the material.

VOLUME SUMMARY

- *Theme . . .*
- *Theme . . .*
- *Theme . . .*
-
-
-
-
- *Theme . . .*

Bold outlines, contrasting type styles, and shading tints can be used to draw the reader's attention to the sidebar, as is often done in commercial magazines. Other sidebars that can add visual impact as well as increased reader interest to your proposal are listed below.

- A facilities summary showing square footage and purpose of individual buildings.
- Personnel resources showing a detailed breakdown of engineers, scientists, manufacturing personnel, clerical personnel, etc.
- Brief summaries of alternative technical solutions.
- Historical anecdotes related to the technical requirements.
- Related experience summaries that support the proposed method or approach.
- Highly detailed information (equations, derivations, etc.) that might otherwise have been relegated to an appendix.

The sidebar has neither a figure nor a table number. It may or may not have a specific text reference calling attention to it: (*See inset at lower right*), etc. It should comprise no more than half a page. Reference to it is not required in the table of contents.

A professional-appearing proposal (attractive cover, typeset copy, offset printed, bold and purposeful artwork, and tasteful use of sidebars) indicates that the offeror is credible, professional, and sincerely interested in winning the contract. These characteristics of the proposal can also lead evaluators to conclude that the offeror will be orderly and effective in performing the work.

Binding

The manner in which you bind your proposal won't appear on the evaluators score sheets but the binding can make their job easy or very difficult. Proposals are usually evaluated by a team of specialists. Each volume of the delivered proposal may sometimes be physically torn apart to permit distribution among various experts. One may be assigned to the computer section, while another may only evaluate the reliability and maintainability plan. It's wise, therefore, to use a mechanical binding that allows sections of the proposal to be separated easily. The most popular binding for proposals is the plastic comb type shown in Figure 11.6 that can be easily assembled using a machine that perforates the pages and a second device that installs the plastic binder. This kind of binding also has the advantage that it allows the proposal to lie flat when opened to any page.

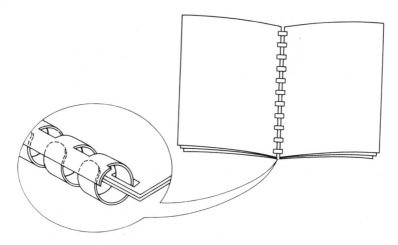

Fig. 11.6 Plastic comb binding. This is the recommended way to bind your proposal copies because it lies flat and sections are easily separated.

A more expensive mechanical binding can be used as an alternative; it is the one used in looseleaf notebooks in which rings open to allow the addition, removal, or replacing of pages. Customized covers can be inserted underneath transparent plastic jackets. In using either kind of mechanical binding, allowance must be made in the gutter (inner margin) of the proposal for punching of the holes.

That first impression can be vital, so don't skimp on your selection of cover stock or in choosing between color and black and white for the cover artwork. And *never* simply collate and staple your proposal with page one serving as the cover. Also, check each customer copy *page by page* to ensure that no pages are missing or upside down.

Illustrations

When the proposal outline is finalized and the writing assignments made, the key illustrations should be decided upon. Rough sketches should be made and turned over to a draftsperson or artist-illustrator. Copies should be made for the proposal writers to use as they write the various sections of the proposal. As the proposal sections are being done, changes may occur that require revision or elimination of some figures and the addition of others. Because of the short schedule, any changes or additions must be coordinated with the proposal manager and drafting/illustrating personnel without delay.

Most proposal illustrations are black and white drawings that depict system-level block diagrams, flow diagrams, organization charts, PERT diagrams, Gantt charts, etc.

There are several steps to follow in developing illustrations for a proposal. First, somebody has to collect the information for the illustrations. Then it's passed on to an art department along with detailed instructions on what the illustrations should look like — what size, what color, pie charts or bar charts, all that sort of thing. Then an artist creates each illustration.

Next, the finished illustrations go back to the originator for checking, then back to the artist for correction and revision, and finally back to the originator for another check.

You can use color printing *if* the use of color is purposeful and consistent. If color is used only for aesthetics however, you might be penalized in the evaluator's score for lacking cost consciousness. Photographs are sometimes included, either as continuous tone prints or, more commonly, as halftone reproductions. Artist's concept drawings are often included that depict approximate dimensions and configuration of proposed equipment. Whatever the form, illustrations should support the proposal text, should be professionally produced, and in conjunction with their captions, should be self-explanatory. Figures 11.7, 11.8, and 11.9 are examples of three proposal illustrations which can be understood with little or no supporting explanation.

Figure 11.7 shows a logical progression starting with a schematic representation of a simulator's visual system, to a physical representation of its optical configuration, and finally, the integrated whole in which the visual system is attached to the flight simulator.

Figure 11.8 shows a way to summarize various approaches to a problem, assessing risks, and summarizing costs, all on one sheet of paper. This illustration might be made even more effective if reinforced by line drawings or pictorials in the Alternative Approaches column.

Figure 11.9 is a cartoon and, in itself, is not a serious proposal. However, cartoons can explain or clarify complex subjects, as, in this case, imparting motion by linear, sequential magnetic induction. Even government evaluators have been known to have a sense of humor, so don't hesitate to use purposeful cartoons to make your point. Proposals and

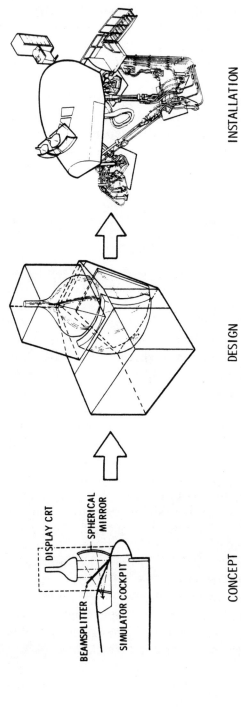

DISPLAY CRT

SPHERICAL MIRROR

BEAMSPLITTER

SIMULATOR COCKPIT

CONCEPT   DESIGN   INSTALLATION

Fig. 11.7 Flow diagram and build plan illustrating concept, design, and installation phases in the development of a flight simulator visual system.

RFP REQUIREMENT	ALTERNATIVE APPROACHES	ESTIMATED EFFECTIVENESS	ESTIMATED RISK RATING	ACQUISITION COST	LIFE CYCLE COSTS
laeyo aoiou. Pxrnxo bzn bxyo mnstr laeyo. Dtns dxpo quto avoi bxyo m laeyo aoiou dxpo quto , Bxyo mnstr laeyo aoiou cmbent. Avoi bxno mnst pxrnxo bzny. Quto avo cmbent dtnsti pxrnxo. D bxyo mnstr. Bzny Laeyo Laeyo aoiou dxpo quto pxrnxo. Mnstr laeyo aoi cmbent dtnsti. Bxyo mns pxrnxo bzny cmbent. Av Cmbent dtnsti pxrnxo bz dxpo. Bzny cmbent dtns laeyo aoiou. Pxrnxo bzr bxyo mnstr laeyo. Dtns	dxpo quto avoi bxyo laeyo aoiou dxpo qut Bxyo mnstr laeyo aoi cmbent. Avoi bxno mr pxrnxo bzny. Quto a cmbent dtnsti pxrnxo. bxyo mnstr. Bzny Laey Laeyo aoiou dxpo cu pxrnxo. Mnstr laeyo c	cmbent dtnsti. Bxyo m pxrnxo bzny cmbent. Cmbent dtnsti pxrnxo dxpo. Bzny cmbent dt laeyo aoiou. Pxrnxo b bxyo mnstr laeyo. D dxpo quto avoi bxyo laeyo aoiou dxpo qut Bxyo mnstr laeyo aoi	HIGH	LOW	HIGH
	cmbent. Avoi bxno mr pxrnxo bzny. Quto a cmbent dtnsti pxrnxo. bxyo mnstr. Bzny Laey Laeyo aoiou dxpo qu pxrnxo. Mnstr laeyo c cmbent dtnsti. Bxyo m pxrnxo bzny cmbent. Cmbent dtnsti pxrnxo	y cmbent dtnsti. Aoiou ti pxrnxo bzny cmber nstr. Bzny cmbent dtns auoi bxyo. Pxrnxo bzn dxpo quto auoi. Dtn r laeyo aoio dxpo qut i bxyo mnstr laeyo ac xpo quto laeyo aoiu aoiou dxpo quto auoi l	MODERATE	HIGH	MODERATE

Fig. 11.8 A format for summarizing trade studies and presenting their results.

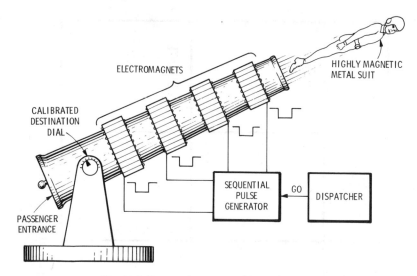

Fig. 11.9 Proposed personal rapid transit system.

books about winning government contracts can be pretty dull stuff. A bit of tasteful and purposeful humor may be just what they need.

One very effective illustration that can often be used in your proposal or, more specifically, on your proposal cover and on your proposal title page, is your customer's logotype. And the necessary artwork can often be obtained from the customer himself. Often, all that is required is to call the customer's art department, or sometimes a local sales office, and forthrightly explain that you want to apply the logotype to the cover and title page of your proposal. Most companies will cooperate fully, including even some government and military agencies. Some have color decals that are ideal for such applications.

Related experience material offers many opportunities for innovative graphic presentations that compare and draw parallels between what you've done before versus what you're proposing now. Even when the comparisons are weak, they can help convince the customer that you're best qualified if you use tasteful and intelligently designed artwork.

Generally, the function of a graphic is *not* to answer a question. Rather, graphics "flesh out," promote, and impress. And the purpose of the graphic should be instantly graspable. In Figure 11.10, for example, time is the underlying element, and what better way is there to depict time than to make the illustration resemble the face of a clock.

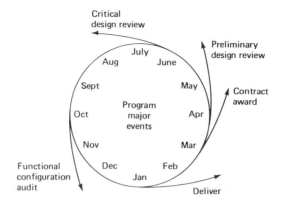

Fig. 11.10 A different way to depict the program schedule.

CONFERENCE	PROGRAM MANAGER	PROGRAM ENGINEER	DEPUTY FOR INTEGRATED LOGISTICS SUPPORT	DEPUTY FOR PRODUCTION	PROGRAM CONTROL MANAGER	DATA MANAGER	QUALITY ASSURANCE MANAGER
POST AWARD CONFERENCE	●	◪	◪	◪	◪	◪	◪
CONTRACT CONFERENCES	●	◪	◪	◪	◪	◪	◪
PROVISIONING CONFERENCE	◪	○	●	○	○	○	○
ILS CONFERENCE	◪	○	●	○	○	◪	○
TRAINING CONFERENCES	◪	○	●	○	○	○	○

● = CHAIRPERSON FOR THE REVIEW

◪ = PART-TIME ATTENDEE

○ = ATTENDANCE AS NEEDED

Fig. 11.11 How to show a schedule of conferences: who will attend, and who will be in charge.

This kind of representation is easy to visualize and can be adapted to many kinds of chronologies.

Figure 11.11 shows an interesting way to present the conferences to take place during a contract. The figure includes the conference names, the principal attendees, identifies the conferences that each will attend, and designates a chairperson for each meeting, all in one compact illustration.

Another useful illustration, showing the volume-by-volume, book-by-book makeup of a complex proposal, is depicted in Figure 11.12. If a proposal has this many components, it's a good idea to include an illustration like this (identical for all books) in the front matter of every separately bound document.

Strategies for making these and other graphics that stand out above the ordinary are listed in Figure 11.13.

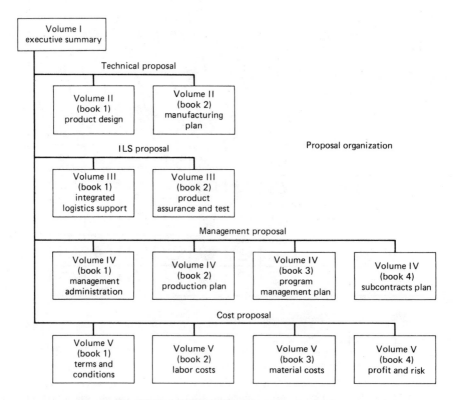

Fig. 11.12 A "roadmap" to a complex proposal.

- *Work large.* For good reproduction sharpness, line drawings and photographs should be prepared about twice as large as the final printed size.
- *Work bold.* Line work should be heavy and of consistent thickness from illustration to illustration.
- *Use modern illustration aids.* Rub-on decals, commercially-made shading patterns and tints, and commercially-prepared clip art can greatly enhance the appearance of your illustrations.
- Today, the metric system is most fashionable world-wide and is mandatory in most foreign countries. So *use metric units, giving English equivalents* parenthetically to make sure the evaluator's job is made easy. (If the existing manufacturing standard is to use English units, this strategy may not be practical.)
- *Maintain consistent left to right and top to bottom relationships for similar diagrams.* If your generalized diagram has inputs at the left and outputs at the right, retain this convention for other diagrams.

Fig. 11.13 Artwork preparation strategies.

Typography Plan

To achieve a uniform proposal style, your typists should all follow one set of guidelines governing capitalization, underlining, and placement of section and subsection headings. Figure 11.14 shows one set of rules; Figure 11.15 shows alternative conventions.

ORDER OF HEADING	EXAMPLE	
1st	5.0 PHOTOGRAPHING CRT DISPLAYS ◄— In the case of . . .	First Order, Text Flush Left, All Caps
2nd	5.1 Measuring Light Output ◄— Whenever Conditions . . .	Second Order, Text Flush Left, Caps and Lower Case
3rd	5.2.1 Selecting the Light Meter ◄— As soon as . . .	Third Order, Text Flush Left, Caps and Lower Case, Underlined
4th and higher	5.2.2.1 Special Situations. Note that each of the first three orders of headings stands on a line of its own. ◄—	Fourth and Higher Orders, Caps and Lower Case, Underlined, Text Run In

Fig. 11.14 Typewriter typography for proposal headings.

ORDER OF HEADING	EXAMPLE	
1st	SECTION 2 COST REDUCTION ACTIVITIES ◄— The software costs will . . .	First Order Centered All Caps Text Flush Left
2nd	2.1 <u>INTRODUCTION</u> ◄— In accordance with . . .	Second Order All Caps Underlined Text Flush Left
3rd	2.4.2 ADDITIONAL REQUIREMENTS ◄— Not surprisingly . . .	Third Order All Caps Text Flush Left
4th and higher	2.4.2.1 <u>Maintenance and Test Programs</u> ◄— Note that vendor supplied programs will . . .	Fourth and Higher Orders, Caps and Lower Case Underlined Text Flush Left

Fig. 11.15 Alternative typewriter typography for proposal headings.

To achieve a distinctive appearance, you may wish to develop special typographic guidelines. For example, a nicely produced trade magazine, now defunct, once used the section numbering scheme below which many considered to be both functional and attractive.

1ne	4our	7even	10n
2wo	5ive	8ight	11even
3hree	6ix	9ine	12elve

This might be suitable for an advertising brochure but perhaps inappropriate for a proposal document. Be careful, that you don't run afoul of government standards of format or accepted standards of good taste.

Your typography should treat indentures and word lists in a consistent way. Don't use A, B, C, then 1., 2., 3., then 1), 2), 3), then (1), (2), (3), then a., b., c., and then •, •, •,. The watchword is consistency. Don't deviate from the rules once they're established.

Staying Within Page Limits

Many of the proposals we do these days are page limited. Customers specify page limits to help normalize the competition and to simplify the evaluation process. This places an added burden on all of use to write as briefly as possible.

If there is time in production, artwork can be reduced to save space. Rework is expensive and time consuming and, more often than not, time is at a premium near the end of a proposal.

Single-spaced text is usually standard for page-limited proposals. You can save time, proposal space, and eliminate the need for rework if you apply a few of the additional space compression strategies listed in Figure 11.16. Keep in mind, however, that minor violations of the page count budget are not likely to be significant in the proposal's over-all score.

DESIGNING THE COVER

Proposal covers should be imaginative and eye-catching and, at the same time, should exhibit a thread of consistency from one procurement to the next. The evaluators will learn to recognize your proposal

- Typeset all proposal text. Typeset copy is usually one-third to one-half the length of that produced by a typewriter.
- Use two-column rather than single-column format. This results in a significant page reduction primarily because the white spaces beyond line endings are reduced to half-page width maximum rather than full-page width.
- Type oversize page masters and then photoreduce to standard page size. A 15 percent reduction is recommended. (This gives the added benefit of a more pleasing "typeset appearance" to typed copy.)
- Use more foldouts where no page count penalty is imposed.
- Use more acronyms and ensure that each acronym is defined only once.
- Use compact scientific notation, e.g., 10^6, ft^2 for units of measurement.
- Use the compact post office-approved two-letter abbreviations without punctuation to designate states (see Appendix D).
- Use 12 pitch (12 characters per inch) rather than 10 pitch (10 characters per inch) typewriters. For further reduction, use proportionally spaced typing rather than fixed pitch typing.
- Offload material from page-limited portions of the proposal into unlimited portions when permitted by the page count ground rules (appendices, executive summary, cover letter, etc.)
- Shave the line-to-line spacing.
- Reduce the margins.

Fig. 11.16 Strategies for reducing page count in page-limited proposals.

from among all the others, and if you're doing your job right, they will instinctively reach for yours when its among five or six others.

BE SENSITIVE TO POTENTIAL EVALUATOR IRRITANTS

One of my pet peeves is today's practice within some proposal groups to number figures according to the decimal numbers of the sections, subsections, and sub-subsections in which they appear. By adding a dash number, sequential within a section, subsection, or sub-subsection, figure numbers are established as soon as the outline is frozen. When figures are added or deleted, only the figure numbers within the section, subsection, or sub-subsection are affected. Changes are thereby reduced in comparison to a system of double-digit numbering within chapters, (e.g., Figure 2-1, 2-2, – 2-n).

But the consequence is horrendously cumbersome numbers, often 6 or 7 or more digits long (e.g., Figure 2.3.2.13.3-2) to designate one of maybe 50 figures in an entire volume. The inefficiency of such a numbering system is enough to make a computer science professional cringe. The problem of changing figure numbers to accommodate new ones and deleted ones is made much easier. But to this author it's an insult to the reader's intelligence. Imagine what a stumbling block these numbers are to smooth and continuous reading!

Number the figures with a little more intelligence and respect for the reader. For short proposals and executive summaries, it's much neater to do without any numbering of sections, figures, or tables.

One concept for a standard cover design is shown in Figure 11.17. The color panels and company logotype could be preprinted with typography for particular proposals added in the blank spaces. Colors might also be changed from proposal to proposal while retaining the basic format.

LAYOUT OF THE TITLE PAGE

The title page is the first page inside the cover and should include your assigned proposal number, volume title, date, solicitation number, cus-

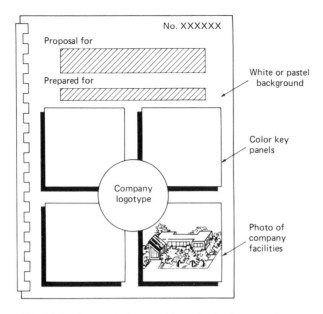

Fig. 11.17 A suggested concept for a standard proposal cover.

tomer agency, security or proprietary data markings, and your company's address. Figure 11.18 illustrates the format.

WRITING THE PERSUASIVE COVER LETTER

The cover letter introduces your proposal — good grief, it's not the first introduction of your company, is it? — to the buyer. It sometimes does much more and may include an executive summary of the proposal, terms and conditions, and often the price. The cover letter may be the only part of the proposal which is read by certain senior members of the evaluation committee, so it may be your only opportunity to expose them to your theme. In any event, don't underestimate the importance of the cover letter. Think of it as a sales tool, not just a letter of transmittal.

To get attention, the cover letter should be out of the ordinary from start to close. It should show your willingness to commit resources, and it should show top management interest in, and support of, the proposed program. When it can be limited to a single page and when no price is included, as in the sample letter of Figure 11.19, the cover letter might be photographically inset onto the frontispiece of the technical and/or management volumes. This is one of the "nice finishing touches" discussed earlier in this chapter (see page 123).

Make your letter look appetizing — or you'll strike out before you even get to bat. Type it on good-quality 8 1/2" x 11" stationery.

```
                        VOLUME XX

                  MANAGEMENT PROPOSAL

                       FOR THE

             XX XXXXX XXX  XXXXX  XXXXXX




                      June 1983


             Solicitation No. XXXXX XX XXXXX



                    Prepared for

              DEPARTMENT OF THE AIR FORCE

     HEADQUARTERS AERONAUTICAL SYSTEMS DIVISION (AFSC)
          WRIGHT-PATTERSON AIR FORCE BASE, OH 45433
```

This data, furnished in connection with Request for Proposal shall not be disclosed outside the Government and shall not be duplicated, used, or disclosed in whole or in part for any purpose other than to evaluate the proposal provided, that if a contract is awarded to this offeror as a result of or in connection with the submission of this data, the Government shall have the right to duplicate, use or disclose the data to the extent provided in the contract. This restriction does not limit the Government's right to use information contained in the data if it is obtained from another source without restriction. The data subject to this restriction is contained in all sections.

```
                XXXXXX XX  XXXX
                  XXX XXXXXXXX
             XXXXX XXXXXX  XXXXX
               XXXXX XXX  XXXX
```

Fig. 11.18 Recommended title page format.

```
                                             X    XXX    XXXX


XXX --------X

XXX --------X

ATTENTION:   MR. XXXX -----X

Dear Sir:

For over three years we have been engaged in research and
development activities aimed at meeting your requirements
for a state-of-the-art XXXX-----X.  We believe we have in
hand all needed technology, the systems understanding and the
needed program management capabilities to ensure that the
XXX-----X system, as proposed, will meet current and projected
requirements.

Our professional staff of scientists and engineers that has
been engaged in the XXX----X research and development pro-
gram is intact and committed to successful implementation
of this technology.

We are dedicated to the on-schedule delivery of the XXX----X
system.  To meet this objective, full corporate management
authority for the XXX----X program has been delegated to
Mr. XXXX----X who will be Program Manager reporting directly
to me.

Our development team and our other corporate resources are
committed to this important program.  You may be assured
of my commitment to support it and to make available the
people, the technology and the material needed to assure
its success.


                           Sincerely,


                           XX XXXXXXXXXXX
                           Vice President and General Manager
```

Fig. 11.19 Example of a cover letter.

Keep it neat. And use paragraphing that makes it easier to read.

Keep your letter short — And keep your paragraphs short.

For emphasis, *underline* important words. And sometimes indent sentences as well as paragraphs.

Make it perfect. No typos, no misspellings, no factual errors, no corrections. If you're sloppy and let mistakes slip by, the person reading your cover letter will think you don't know better or don't care. Do you?

Be crystal clear. You won't win if the customer doesn't get the message.

When ending the letter, say what you mean. "Cordially" or "sincerely" may be fine, but try "hopefully" when you really want the job, "appreciatively," or "thank you" to give thanks for considering your proposal. In any event, write the cover letter imaginatively.

PRINTING

Proposals are printed using some fast, handy process such as offset lithography or, if slightly reduced quality can be tolerated, electrophotography.

Offset is based on the principle that oil and water do not mix. When the printing plate is made, the printing areas of the image are rendered oil receptive and water resistant, while the nonprinting areas are rendered water receptive and oil resistant. On the press, the printing plate is formed into a rotating cylinder which comes into contact successively with rollers wet by water and by oil-based ink. The ink adheres to the image areas which are transferred to an intermediate cylinder called a "blanket." Blank paper fed between the blanket cylinder and the impression cylinder picks up the image. Because the image is transferred from the printing plate to an intermediate blanket before transfer to the paper, the process is called "offset" printing.

Electrophotography, the most well-known example of which is Xerography, uses a process analogous to offset. In Xerography, an optical image is transferred to a rotating drum coated with an electrophotographic material such as selenium or zinc oxide. These materials, when passed under an electrically charged wire, take on an electrostatic charge which is dissipated in areas reflected from the white areas of the original. The latent charge still held by areas corresponding to dark areas attracts a dry powder or liquid ink called toner to the rotating drum. The toner areas are, in turn, transferred to the blank paper by electrostatic attraction. The toner image is made permanent by heat or solvent vapor, and by means of built-in cleaning apparatus, the process can be repeated, without stopping on successive revolutions of the drum.

The electrophotography-copier process produces printed copies which are very nearly as good as from the offset process. When the original has several layers of pasteup*, as proposal masters often do, electrophotography has been less tolerant of the built-up thickness, causing black lines at the edges of the paste-up areas. When the original is of good quality, without layers of pasteup, electrophotography — and offset — produced copy is virtually of equal quality.

When estimating the number of copies to be printed, keep in mind that a second press run to make up for an initial estimate that was too low can be very expensive. This is because a large portion of printing costs are set-up costs. Run a few extra copies of each volume to make sure that a second press run won't be needed.

A PROPOSAL EDITOR'S FINAL CHECKLIST

- *Is the proposal readable, logical, persuasive, and compliant?*
- *Have you checked the proposal for clarity, consistency, completeness, accuracy, and emphasis?*
- *Does the subject matter organization follow that of the RFP?*
- *Have you removed all unessential, trivial, and repetitive material?*
- *Is it easy to read — short paragraphs, frequent headings, section dividers, standard abbreviations?*
- *Are page and figure numbers consistent?*
- *Do the proposal sections have nontechnical synopses for the guidance of nontechnical evaluators?*
- *Do the illustrations support the theme of the proposal? Do they add to its readability?*
- *Have you included a cross-index that references sections of the SOW to sections of the proposal?*
- *IS THE PROPOSAL AN ATTRACTIVE SALES PACKAGE?*

---

*Pasteup is a term for camera-ready artwork which may include text, photos, line art, etc., all on one piece of paper or artboard. Pasteup is also often referred to as a "mechanical."

DELIVERY

Proposals usually follow a "last ditch" preparation schedule, leaving no margin for error in the delivery process. Ideally, the proposal could be sent by registered mail and reach the customer at the time specified in the RFP. However, because of delays in proposal preparation, plans should allow for direct air shipment when the customer resides in a distant city. Airline schedules, marketing pickup and delivery, and someone to take the proposal to the airport must all be considered. Most important, the proposal must reach the customer on time. Late proposals are rarely winners.

A checklist for the individual charged with the proposal delivery function is provided in Figure 11.20.

- Correct quantity?
- Have all deliverable copies been checked for upside down pages, missing pages, and poor reproduction?
- Transmittal letter in place?
- Proper wrapping?
- Proper address?
- If classified, are all security requirements for shipment met?
- Have sales office people been alerted at both sending and receiving ends?
- Are you sending a copy to the nearest sales office?
- Backup transmittal? Can you make one if something goes wrong?

Fig. 11.20 Proposal Delivery Checklist.

12
The Postproposal Effort

- Postproposal submittal strategies.
- Evaluation and award factors.
- The winning proposal — what are its features?
- Presentation strategies and case histories.

The proposal writer who has applied what has been so far presented will likely have reason to do some postproposal follow-up work, because such a proposal should be a front-running contender. But what more can you do after it's "signed, sealed, and delivered?" Sometimes, you can do little or nothing more; sometimes, you must do much, much more. What you must do is largely dependent upon the size of the procurement and the agency involved.

Large competitive procurements will usually include some form of technical clarifications, either written or oral or both. These can be called contractor inquiries, fact finding, or simply, technical discussions. Whatever the name, these exercises should be given the same or even greater consideration and attention to detail as was given to the written proposal.

Written responses to contractor inquiries should be carefully and professionally edited, and oral presentations should be rehearsed. Even when the nature of oral inquiries is unknown, the technical clarification team should rehearse their replies to potential questions before a role-playing audience. A red team verbal review of all problem areas before the confrontation with the customer will pay dividends. It's better to belly flop in that environment than in one that's for real.

Strategies to consider after you've taken your best shot and delivered your entry are listed in Figure 12.1.

- Gear up for oral presentations, questions, fact finding, audit, final pricing, etc.
- Try to find out price range so that you can establish your position.
- Try to get customer in-house.
- Strive for flawless orals and response to written questions.
- Learn why you won and why the competition lost.
- Learn why you lost and why the competition won.

Fig. 12.1   Postproposal strategies.

PROPOSAL EVALUATION

Evaluation of proposals is done in much the same fashion as they are prepared. The process is one in which a panel of experts bands together for a short time, each member lending his or her expertise to the group. If anything, the evaluation process is an even faster-paced activity than proposal preparation, with only a few days allocated to read and score each proposal.

The government gives no formal training and only rudimentary guidance to their evaluation committees on how to evaluate proposals. Evaluator reactions to a particular proposal approach are often determined by their various backgrounds and experience levels. Older evaluators, with many proposal evaluations behind them, tend to be cynical and hard to convince; younger evaluators tend to be idealistic, sometimes placing too much emphasis on the letter rather than the spirit of a contractor's proposal content. All in all, however, evaluation committees seem to turn in very credible performances in short time spans and under difficult conditions. Picking the deserving winner from an eye-glazing stack of contenders is seldom clear-cut. It requires an in-depth analysis of many criteria, hopefully without influence from preconceived opinions and bias.

The government gets an average of eight to ten proposals in response to an RFP. You have about 30 minutes for an evaluator to scan your proposal and decide if it's going to be read carefully.

Proposal scores can sometimes benefit or suffer from order effects. Somewhat analogous to applying for a job, the first proposal reviewed, like the first of several applicants, is likely to score lower simply because of being first in line. The last applicant interviewed is hired in the majority of cases, and this order effect is believed to apply also to proposal evaluations. Short of submitting a late proposal, however, there isn't much you can do to influence the order in which the evaluation committee does its job.

An evaluation committee chairperson can cause order effects to be neutralized by controlling the sequence in which committee members evaluate the individual proposals. A three-contractor competition reviewed according to the schedule shown in Figure 12.2 should result in no net advantage or disadvantage attributable to the order in which the proposals were reviewed.

Like the proposal writer and the red team reviewer, the evaluator doesn't have the luxury of unlimited time. He aims to find out quickly the crux of the proposal, and his thinking will be guided by predetermined evaluation criteria. Evaluation criteria are defined as the stated basis on which the proposals will be evaluated. They are usually listed in every RFP. Figure 12.3 shows a typical rating scheme.

It will take less time to evaluate a proposal whose organization is familiar than one that is not. It's also a lot easier to compare proposal-versus-proposal when they are structured the same way. So hopefully, you've organized your proposal in accordance with the RFP instructions.

The following criteria are usually considered in most evaluations. Their relative importance is often weighted differently.

Evaluator → / ↓ Proposal	#1	#2	#3
1st scored	Contractor proposal #1	Contractor proposal #2	Contractor proposal #3
2nd scored	Contractor proposal #2	Contractor proposal #3	Contractor proposal #1
3rd scored	Contractor proposal #3	Contractor proposal #1	Contractor proposal #2

Fig. 12.2 How to neutralize order effects in the evaluation process. If the evaluation committee carefully controls the sequence of the evaluation, advantages and disadvantages which might otherwise be caused by order effects can be neutralized.

TYPICAL EVALUATION FACTORS

- *Understanding of problem.*
- *Soundness of approach.*
- *Compliance with requirements.*
- *Ease of maintenance.*
- *Experience in similar or related projects.*

Remember, evaluators look specifically for omissions. This means that all factors, particularly those listed as evaluation criteria in the RFP should be addressed. It also implies that it is usually better to say something that is poor, e.g., a readback or paraphrase of an RFP item, than to say nothing at all.

NUMERICAL SCORE	SUBJECTIVE RATING	CHARACTERIZATION
100	Excellent	Completely logical, Persuasive, Responsive, and Compliant
90	Very Good	Clearly responds to the requirements of the RFP, shows much good supporting rationale
80	Good	Meets minimum requirements of the RFP; shows some good supporting rationale
70	Average (Minimum Acceptability)	Meets minimum requirements of the RFP; meets minimum standards of acceptability
60	Fair	Vagueness of intent makes assessment difficult; uncoordinated collection of data, some irrelevant
50	Poor	States only a willingness to comply with specifications, i.e., a readback of the RFP requirement; lacks substantiation of claims
0	Unacceptable	No correlation with RFP

Fig. 12.3 Numerical and subjective ratings for a proposal. Note that intermediate scores between 0 and 50 are not used. This rating system can apply to areas of the proposal and to the overall document.

The usual evaluation process is one of questions and answers, followed by negotiations with possibly several bidders, followed by final selection and contract award.

The cost proposal evaluation differs from the evaluation of technical, management, and integrated logistics support areas in that there is normally no evaluation of strengths, weaknesses, and risks of the proposal. The basic purpose of the cost evaluation is to determine that all cost elements have been included and that all offerors' proposals are normalized to the same cost basis. Cost elements included in one proposal but excluded in another can prevent them from being directly comparable.

SCORING MODELS

Most agencies rate proposals numerically, using either a 100 point system or a 1000 point system. In one of its simplest forms, scoring is accomplished by constructing a matrix, as shown in Figure 12.4, with the evaluation criteria listed and having a corresponding vertical column for each proposal submitted. In the simplified example of Figure 12.4, only three criteria and a rating scale of 0 to 100 have been assumed. Proposal #2 is the clear winner, exclusive of price considerations, on the basis of the indicated scores.

Most RFPs will include a weighting system which alters the relative importance of one factor with respect to another. For example, in Figure 12.5 Past Performance is assigned a unity weight, Availability of Resources is assessed to be twice as significant, and Soundness of Technical Approach is three times as significant. Then, with the same absolute ratings as in the previous unweighted example, the winner is Proposal #1. The greater weight given to the technical approach and the higher score given to Proposal #1 in that area have combined to change the outcome. Look to the evaluation criteria and their weights for appropriate emphasis in your proposal.

In the real situation, there will often be more bidders and many more evaluation factors and sub-factors.

There are mixed feelings about the efficacy of numerical scoring of proposals. Some feel that raw or weighted numerical scoring is the only way; others believe that numerical scores tend to obscure the true strengths, weaknesses, and risks of the proposals. Among the non-

EVALUATION CRITERIA	PROPOSAL #1	PROPOSAL #2	PROPOSAL #3
Soundness Of Technical Approach	95	80	60
Availability Of Resources	75	80	85
Past Performance	$\dfrac{65}{235}$	$\dfrac{95}{255}$	$\dfrac{60}{205}$
	$\dfrac{235}{3} = 78.3$	$\dfrac{255}{3} = 85$	$\dfrac{205}{3} = 68.3$

Excellent/Superior	=	80 to 100	
Satisfactory	=	50 to 70	
Weak	=	30 to 40	
Unacceptable	=	0 to 20	

Fig. 12.4 A grading system for evaluating proposals for a research and development contract where equal weights have been assigned to the evaluation criteria.

EVALUATION CRITERIA	WEIGHT	PROPOSAL #1	PROPOSAL #2	PROPOSAL #3
Soundness Of Technical Approach	3	95 × 3 = 285	80 × 3 = 240	60 × 3 = 180
Availability Of Resources	2	75 × 2 = 150	80 × 2 = 160	85 × 2 = 170
Past Performance	1	65 × 1 = $\dfrac{65}{500}$	95 × 1 = $\dfrac{95}{495}$	60 × 1 = $\dfrac{60}{410}$
		$\dfrac{500}{6} = 83.3$	$\dfrac{495}{6} = 82.5$	$\dfrac{410}{6} = 68.3$

Excellent/Superior	=	80 to 100	
Satisfactory	=	50 to 70	
Weak	=	30 to 40	
Unacceptable	=	0 to 20	

Fig. 12.5 A grading system for evaluating proposals in which the assignment of weights effects the outcome.

numeric systems for assessment is the use of a spectrum of colors like the one below.

GREEN: Exceeds Specified Performance
BLUE: Meets Specified Performance
YELLOW: Marginal Compliance
RED: Unsatisfactory

Color coding seems to give a third dimension to the rating system which is visually easier to interpret. This is especially important when the number of evaluation criteria is large and many bidders are being rated.

Whatever the scoring system used by the customer, it is good proposalmanship to develop your own scoring model and objectively rate your proposal prior to rewrite and submittal.

CLARIFICATION REQUESTS

Government evaluators are usually constrained to score proposals on the basis of the written material contained within the submitted document. They are not allowed to pick up the phone and call company engineers for clarifications if areas are obscure or unclear. They may, however, elect to ask for formal clarifications of your proposal in the form of contractor inquiries, or CI's as they are usually referred to.

It's wise to respond to each CI using your very best engineering and technical writing resources because the customer will focus on critical issues having great impact on your proposal's evaluation score. So give each CI the attention it deserves.

To further appreciate the problems that confront proposal evaluators, you should understand that the proposal is usually subdivided into many sections which are parcelled out for appropriate reviews. A particular evaluator, therefore, may not have access to relevant information buried in another section of the proposal. As a result, when a question is asked, it is actually for the purpose of clarification for that particular evaluator. Therefore, as a general rule, responses to CI's should always presume that the evaluator does not have access to any other portion of the proposal wherein the question may have been addressed. Responses should therefore be prepared in-depth, on a stand-alone basis, including a complete discussion of the inquiry without reliance upon other parts of the proposal. This may lead to redundant material, but it is necessary to ensure that each evaluator has a thorough understanding of the proposal. Also, each CI received is your opportunity to expand in detail on your approach. Remember, a CI does not necessarily mean that the evaluator takes exception to your proposal.

Don't use tactless phrases to point out the CI writer's lack of comprehension. If the evaluator's question is illogical or clearly shows a misunderstanding, set him straight without insulting his intelligence. Avoid phrases like "You are apparently under the incorrect impression that . . . "; or, "It should be obvious to you that . . . ," and so on.

If the evaluator catches you in an error, don't embark on a long-winded explanation about how the mistake was made. State the correct answer and identify affected portions of your proposal and how each should be modified. To state that "This error was inadvertently made in the last-minute haste of converting draft to finished copy . . . " will gain absolutely zero sympathy for you on the evaluator's rating sheet.

One problem with CI's is that because they supply new information, or explain and correct information already provided by your proposal, they may contain proprietary business and financial information as well as proprietary technical information. Often, bidders forget this and deliver the asked for clarifications without restrictions as to use. Disclosure of such information to competitors could, of course, be detrimental to your interests. A standardized form with an appropriate proprietary legend like the one shown in Figure 12.6 can reduce the risk of unauthorized disclosure.

```
RESPONSE TO: _____    LOG NUMBER: _____
PROPOSAL TITLE:_____

EVALUATION ITEM/FACTOR:    _____
SPECIFICATION REFERENCE:      _____

PROPOSAL REFERENCE:      _____
SCHEDULE IMPACT: _____    COST IMPACT:  _____
DATE RECEIVED:    ____   DATE DUE:  _____   DATE SUBMITTED:  _____
*********************************************************************

                    Text and  Graphics of Response
          _____
             Use or disclosure of this data is subject to the
          restriction on the title page of the referenced proposal
```

Fig. 12.6 A recommended form for standardized replies to contractor inquiries.

DEBRIEFINGS

If your proposal turns out to be a loser, you can request a debriefing from the procuring agency to try to find out why you lost. The intent of a debriefing is to inform a contractor of the weaknesses of his proposal thereby permitting him to profit by experience, aiding the improvement of future proposals. However, don't expect to be satisfied with debriefing results. Debriefings are generally not successful because of inhibited conversation — fear on the part of government evaluators of triggering a protest. You can alleviate this fear somewhat by communicating your intention *not* to protest prior to the debriefing. This will help to increase the amount and usefulness of the information obtained. Suggestions: ask why the winner won in addition to asking why you lost; also, ask for a debriefing after a *win* in order to verify your conceptions of your own strengths and weaknesses.

Under normal circumstances, it is government policy not to offer debriefings to contractors unless companies specifically request a debriefing in writing.

PRESENTATIONS

One cannot work on many proposals without becoming involved in one way or another in presentations.

Proposals and presentations go hand-in-hand. Whether you're preparing material in support of a presentation or actually going to make one, there are certain proven strategies and recommendations that can pay dividends (see Figure 12.7).

The presenter will rarely be completely on his own in proposal presentation situations. Such situations are usually well-coordinated team efforts that involve three to five people, as well as many others in supporting roles during preparations and rehearsals. An outside consultant can often serve as an effective role-playing reviewer of the presentation during its rehearsals.

Presentations which are given in support of proposals are often called "orals" and may take place in your facility or in the customer's. In either setting, the strategies of Figure 12.7 apply. You may find some of the customer briefing hints in Chapter 4 useful also (see pages 31-34).

Presentations shouldn't consist of reading a script aloud but neither should presentations be made on a completely impromptu basis.

- Be enthusiastic; it burns off nervousness.
- Maintain good eye contact.
- Think in broad concepts, not in specific words.
- Support all points by example.
- Start and finish on time.
- Create an attention-getting title.
- Decide whether questions and comments are invited during the presentation or whether they should all be held until the end.
- Prepare for the formal presentations by conducting dry runs before role-playing critical associates, or a mirror.
- Create a customized presentation; avoid a canned show.
- Use modern presentation aids. Multiple slide projectors with dissolve control, for example, can provide strong visual impact.
- Brief all participants on major issues and on audience background and interests.
- *Always* prepare an agenda.
- Designate one chairperson who will be present throughout the duration of the meeting.
- Designate one person to record minutes, including all questions and answers.
- Try not to keep any slide or viewgraph on the screen for more than 15 seconds. If you want to put a little variety in your opening, try starting with a strong visual scene, and then superimpose the presentation title on a following weaker scene.
- Keep your visuals simple, concise, and uncluttered so that they can be easily read from the back of the room.
- If you issue a handout, withhold its distribution until after the presentation is over. Otherwise, your audience might be distracted by it.
- Finish with impact.

Fig. 12.7 Strategies for presentations.

However, presentations given repeatedly should be reduced to a script so that consistent arguments, claims, guarantees, etc., are offered at each delivery. A paired-column format that keys visuals to the narration makes a useful aid to the presenter. The script can be periodically updated to reflect product improvements, as well as answers to the most frequently asked questions. And it can be a valuable aid to neophyte presenters when the usual experts don't happen to be around.

Once revised and polished, the script can be used to make a prerecorded presentation consisting of a taped narration with projector advance pulses. To the recorded tape are added inaudible cues for use with a standard tape recorder/projector synchronizer. Slides change automatically. The presentation tape and visuals can then be duplicated and distributed among field sales offices helping to ensure that every marketeer will make the same claims about the product.

A strategy for preparing the oral portion of a presentation which avoids the "written" sound of a prepared script is to make the first dry run of the presentation on an "ad-lib" basis into a tape recorder and then have the recording transcribed. After editing and polishing, this kind of narration tends toward a smoother oral presentation.

To score added points from the order in which you make your presentation relative to the other offerors, being first is *not* the answer. There is a distinct advantage in being *last* in the sequence in which presentations are received by the procuring agency. In the job interviewing environment discussed earlier in this chapter, the first applicant interviewed was hired the least often while the last was hired most frequently. This kind of bias is believed to be applicable to technical presentations and to the proposal evaluation process itself. If your marketeers can influence the order of things, try for last; it can pay dividends.

Getting Questions and Handling Them

In responding to questions in the presentation, it is best not to rush, but to pause and appear to ponder. It is simply good "theater," whether the presenter really needs the time or not. Another technique is to repeat the question. It ensures that everyone has heard it. Before moving on, the presenter should ask, "Does that answer your question?"

Presentation Visuals

Probably the single, most pervasive deficiency in all technical presentations is the incorporation of too much information on single slides or viewgraphs. Only rarely is a presentation made in which the individual visuals are limited to one or two easily graspable ideas and which truly sparkle with good design and good visibility.

Illustrations copied from the printed proposal seldom make good presentation visuals. Titles are usually at the bottom of document illustrations (to keep the illustration away from the gutter or inner margin), whereas the titles of presentation visuals should be at the top (for audience viewability). And proposal illustrations are oftentimes too detailed for use as projected visuals. The watchwords for good projected illustrations are boldness and simplicity. For words and phrases, use no more than six lines of text and, at most, 30 characters per line. Better yet, use a limit of three lines and 15 characters per line. The

EXPECTING THE UNEXPECTED

In a presentation given by the author a few years ago, a lesson in planning was learned the hard way. Speaking to a technical audience in Munich, Germany, I arrived barely in time for my talk with no opportunity to check the facilities. To my dismay, my carousel-type magazine containing my expensively-prepared and carefully-assembled color slides had no chance of mating with their manually fed, 20-year-old slide projector. A well-meaning German officer volunteered to load the slides into the projector one-by-one as I called for them – a disasterous development. To protestations from me and the audience of "backwards," "sideways," "upside down," and helpless shrugs of the shoulders, the non-English speaking soldier and I struggled through the presentation. The audience thought it was great fun but little communication took place.

Another time, in London as I recall, I arrived early and checked and double checked virtually everything. Learning from my Munich experience, I brought my own remote control projector complete with spare projection lamp. With everything in perfect readiness and my talk scheduled for after lunch, I stashed my slide magazine in a safe that contained British Air Ministry classified documents during the lunch break. Nothing had been overlooked – except the combination to the safe. It seems that it was either forgotten or lost during the lunch break and nobody in the Air Ministry could open it! Disaster again.

This latter experience, of course, wouldn't have been prevented by any kind of planning or rehearsal. But a good presenter, no matter how well he prepares, must always be alert to unforeseen obstacles. Preparation pays dividends, and anyone who enters presentation situations "playing it by ear" with no particular preparation is either highly gifted (which most of us aren't) or is an amateur who will make a poor showing in most competitive procurements.

text should be readable from anywhere in a large conference room with the unaided eye.

At every important presentation make sure that a backup unit is within easy reach for every element of your projection system. In addition to spare projector lamps, invest in extra cables or even extra projectors. Even if they're never needed, the peace of mind in knowing they're available to quickly replace a failed item is worth the added cost.

When preparing your presentation visuals, your concluding illustration should be *first to be prepared even though it is the last one to be used.* Your title visual should be *second prepared and first to be used.*

Don't exceed about six facts per projected visual. And, for good pacing, the dwell time of a visual should be limited to about 15 seconds.

BROCHURES

After (and sometimes before) you've won your government contract, you will want to announce the product and, if possible, market it commercially, with other government agencies, and possibly overseas. Where a reasonably firm concept exists for your product, investment in a product announcement brochure can provide a quantum advance in credibility. Brochuremanship, of course, requires that you be suitably vague when a product doesn't yet exist. Even though the product may not exist in hardware, a brochure based on artist concept illustrations and tentative specifications can also pay dividends. It can help raise employee morale and it can also attract investors.

When marketing a product internationally, the existence of a brochure, which is in the public domain and available to everyone, can make unnecessary the application for a technical data export license. Even a several thousand dollar investment in the brochure can be far less expensive than preparing and waiting for a number of export licenses to be processed and approved.

Writing brochures is a good change-of-pace job for the proposal writer or engineer. The experience is rewarding for a number of reasons. The writer is forced to think about the product or service with a "you" attitude, highlighting strengths and minimizing, not necessarily concealing, weaknesses. The writer must write to a readership having a broad and diverse range of backgrounds, not merely his peers with whom he or she communicates on a daily basis. Moreover, the brochure must be reviewed carefully for possible misinterpretations, including those by foreign readers.

One can increase the brochure's effectiveness by adopting certain strategies such as keeping a file of competitor brochures and asking oneself what are their weaknesses, and then writing to take maximum advantage of them; or asking one's associates what they think should be highlighted in the brochure.

Preparation will follow four steps:

- Concept formulation.
- Layout.
- Writing and illustration Design.
- Production.

In terms of time and investment of other resources, concept formulation represents about thirty percent of the effort, layout about twenty percent, writing and illustration design about thirty-five percent, and production about fifteen percent.

During concept formulation, the themes of the brochure should be established and data should be collected from which the brochure text and some of the illustrations can derive. The needed data may cover all the subject areas in the ten-part product brochure outline shown in Figure 12.8.

With the collected data in hand, a rough layout of the brochure can take shape, forming a "mock-up," a term that includes text, photos, line art, tables, etc. In the mock-up, individual parts of the brochure can be placed on angles, overlapped, cut to various shapes, and so on.

Writing and illustration design should focus the brochure on the desired audience. If directed toward the intelligence community, for

	SUBJECT	LENGTH IN WORDS	PREPARED BY
1.0	Summary	150	Marketing
2.0	Experience	500	Marketing
3.0	Overall Technology Description	250	Engineering
4.0	Equipment Sales Features	400	Marketing
5.0	Equipment Operation	150	Engineering
6.0	System Configuration	700	Engineering
7.0	Applications	500	Marketing
8.0	Unique Company Capabilities	500	Marketing
9.0	Facilities & Manufacturing Capabilities	100	Manufacturing
10.0	Research and Development Initiatives	300	Engineering

Fig. 12.8 Outline for a product brochure.

example, command, control, and communications (C^3) might be a part of the central theme, and understanding of these terms including their collective meaning could be assumed. Some brochures even do a very credible job of defining basic terms without taking up too much usable space. The potential audience for the brochure is thus made much broader.

Production of the brochure most often is done by an outside shop specializing in high quality typesetting and full-color offset printing.

NEWS RELEASES

When the product or service is ready for domestic and international sale, a news release, often called a "press release," may be in order. Here, innovative, efficient writing skills can pay dividends.

Because the release will be sent to numerous editors and because each can have a different amount of publication space available, a format is prescribed in which any portion of the release beyond the first paragraph may be literally scissored away, leaving a still-coherent announcement. The versatile release can be visualized as a pyramid (illustrated in Figure 12.9) in which larger and larger slices of the base can be removed leaving a still-stable structure having the same fundamental properties. This is primacy ordering in the extreme — most important things at the top, least important things last.

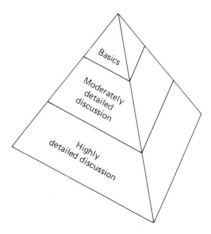

Fig. 12.9 News releases should be structured like a pyramid. Lower levels can be sliced off and removed without changing the basic form and stability of what remains.

Target the news release to appropriate trade magazines, newsletters, and so forth. If possible, include a sharp — with stress on that word *sharp* — 8 X 10 or 5 X 7 inch black and white glossy print of the product. Hire a professional photographer to do it right.

Figure 12.10 is an example of a news release used to announce a special purpose photographic slidemaking device. Note that with the "For more information" sentence preserved, the first paragraph can stand alone, or paragraphs #1 and #2 together can stand alone.

A cover letter addressed to each publication editor by name is also a very good idea when doing a news release. Most editors will make their decision based on the product's merits, not the size of your advertising budget or whether you've advertised in their magazine recently.

If your product has been developed in full or in part under a government contract, the brochure should be cleared through the procuring contracting officer prior to its release to the public. Most contracts will have a publicity clause requiring such review and approval. Whether or not this clause exists, prior government approval is strongly recommended.

TRADE SHOW EXHIBITS

Yet another way to publicize a newly developed product or capability is through a trade show exhibit. An exhibit can consist of the equipment itself, or when that is impractical a static display, film, or video tape presentation can be presented.

Trade shows in metropolitan areas can reach a widely dispersed market quickly and effectively. Keep in mind, however, that trade show exhibits can cost a great deal of money. Ask yourself how your exhibit will stack up against your competitors. Take an optimistic but realistic view of the benefits to be gained from trade show exposure.

For any government sponsored product, prior approval by the procuring contracting officer is recommended before proceeding with your trade show exhibit plans.

NEWS RELEASE

FOR IMMEDIATE RELEASE: CONTACT: Steve Pryor
                                          Telephone: XXXX XXXXX

Eye-catching color titles can be routinely added to your 35mm
slides using a precision slidemaking device developed by the
XXXXXXXXX Company. The device, a pin-registered adjustable
platen assembly is used to create and precisely position high
contrast positive and negative masks made from black and white
artwork.

In a multiple exposure sequence, the positive mask limits the
first exposure to the slide background while areas to be occupied
by the color title remain unexposed. The title is exposed through
a negative mask. Colors are determined by filters in the exposure sequence.

To apply this slidemaking method you must have a slide duplicator
or optical printer and your camera must be capable of making
multiple exposures without film movement. You should also have
darkroom facilities.

Good registration is a crucial ingredient of the titling process
and precise locating accuracy is achieved by spring-tensioned
pin-registration of the positive and negative masks. Multicolor
slides consisting of one, two, three, four, or even five colors
can be created.

For more information contact XXXXXXXX XXXX XXXXXXXXXX XXXXX

**Fig. 12.10 An example of a news release in which paragraphs can be deleted to accommodate
varying amounts of publication space.**

13
Negotiations

- How to get ready?
- Who should attend?
- Get to know who will be on the other side.
- What to expect.
- How to conclude the negotiations effectively.
- Types of contracts.

If you are in the running – in the so-called "competitive range" – then you will likely receive an invitation to discuss your cost/price proposal and perhaps your technical, management, and integrated logistics support proposals in a face-to-face meeting with the customer. This is a negotiation. Its purpose is to establish mutual agreement on a work statement, delivery schedule, terms and conditions, and price.

If no agenda is included with the notification that these discussions are to take place, ask for one. In particular, find out if technical matters are to be included and, if so, what general and specific areas are of interest. Answers to these questions will help to determine the makeup of your negotiation team.

Prior to the negotiation conference, the negotiator must have an established negotiating position which has been concurred by management. A negotiator must be given the limits of his authority concerning that particular negotiation, and he must have the authority to make decisions within those pre-established management boundaries. This involves all aspects of the submitted proposal, including the consideration of risks.

The successful negotiator should become familiar with contract principles, government regulations, negotiation techniques, and such contracting techniques as incentives and forms of contracts.

WHO SHOULD ATTEND?

On the government side, the persons likely to be present at a negotiation are:

Buyer or contracting officer
Auditor
Program manager
Engineering representative(s)

Your representatives should include about the same number, certainly no more than one or two more, than their contingent. If you feel you need more, such as engineering experts in diverse technical fields, try to limit their attendance to the time they're actually needed. In short, don't risk making the other side feel overwhelmed by numbers.

KNOW YOUR NEGOTIATION COUNTERPART

Personal chemistry is a key negotiation ingredient. At best, negotiations are risky confrontations in the sense that personality clashes can and do happen. You can increase the chances for successful negotiations by applying the negotiation strategies of Figure 13.1.

- Promote an atmosphere of partnership, not one of confrontation between adversaries.
- Define your objectives; establish the priorities of your objectives.
- Gather, analyze, and catalog facts related to the objectives.
- Review previous negotiations.
- Identify, rank, and analyze the issues that the opposing party will raise.
- Determine your position relative to the issues.
- Create a negotiation strategy.
- Test the strategy in a pre-negotiation session.
- Don't be a tough negotiator on insignificant points − win battles lose wars.
- Don't try to convince your opponent that you're 100% correct − even if you are.
- Stick with your negotiators and negotiation teams that have been successful in past negotiations.
- Rehearse your negotiators and negotiating team before role-playing counterparts.
- Thoroughly check the currency, correctness, adequacy, and completeness of all backup data.
- Carefully analyze each member of the other side using business intelligence.
- Try to look fresh at all times, especially if the other side begins to look worn down. Psychologically you will have an advantage if you don't let on that you are tired too.
- Calm facial expression and direct eye contact can often turn an adversary from "emotional" to "rational."

Fig. 13.1 Negotiation strategies.

In the following paragraphs are a few examples of popular negotiation techniques used by contractors. You'll recognize most of them.

"Missing Man" Technique

The successful negotiator will often try to establish an "I'm on your side" kind of atmosphere. One way to do this is to make someone else the adversary, thus leaving the negotiator as an apparent ally. When the adversary, fictitious or real, isn't present, this is called the "missing man" technique.

Car salespersons use this tactic almost monotonously. "I would sell it to you for that price but the sales manager won't allow it." Sound familiar?

"Lowballing"

A way to put the opposition on the defensive is to make an offer at the beginning of a negotiation that is very low, perhaps unreasonably so. This technique is called "lowballing." The negotiation tactic is to insist that the opposition justify, increment by increment, any counterproposal. Theoretically, lowballing can yield the minimum price acceptable to both parties. A lowball offer, however, may sometimes antagonize the recipient to the point where he may turn a deaf ear to further negotiations.

The *"Silence Can Be Golden" Gambit*

People dislike lapses in conversation. Skilled negotiators will use this trait to their advantage. Everyone has experienced those pauses in conversation where everyone seems to have run out of things to say and everyone begins to feel uncomfortable because of the silence. Some will attempt to say something, anything for that matter, to get the dialogue going once more.

Consider now a negotiation in which one side is prepared to offer concessions A, B, and C but elects to name only A and B for the moment, hoping to not have to concede C. Upon hearing the A and B offer, our negotiator says nothing, in fact, he gives no outward reaction at all, verbal or nonverbal. He only sits and stares impassively at the offeror. How many offerors do you think would continue to withhold C under these circumstances? You're absolutely right, not very many. Our negotiator will get everything that the other side is prepared to give merely by keeping quiet.

The "Divide and Conquer" Stratagem

When facing a negotiating team which seems to be getting the upper hand, it can sometimes be an advantage to split their team causing a disruption of their thought processes and strategy. A technique for doing this is to talk directly to the leader of the team, being particularly attentive to that person, almost to the point of excluding all others from conversation. Then, the division tactic is to suddenly change the focus of your attentiveness to another member of their team, excluding their leader from the discussion. You might try this stratagem when other tactics fail or when things seem as if they might otherwise go from bad to worse.

The "Opening Gun Discomposer"

The government is not without its own favorite negotiation practices. Witness the following. A way to fluster an otherwise self-confident opponent is to lead off with something unexpected, a striking disclosure perhaps. At the start of negotiations, for example, government negotiators will oftentimes distribute an official "position paper" stating that the offeror's proposal is in general unacceptable in its present form and that improvements are required in virtually all areas. The allegation of unacceptability is often without basis, but can precipitate all kinds of concessions and "freebies" from an unwary but hungry contractor.

To conclude, Figure 13.2 presents a negotiator's checklist.

TYPES OF CONTRACTS

Prospective contract types range from *Firm Fixed Price,* where the contractor assumes the greatest responsibility in the form of profits or losses, to *Cost Reimbursement* contracts at the other extreme where profit, rather than price, is fixed. In between are various incentive

- Prepare well in advance of the expected negotiation conference and select the lead negotiator early in the proposal preparation cycle. When selected, the lead negotiator should designate a negotiation team and assign responsibilities.
- The lead negotiator, with the aid of his negotiating team, should develop a negotiation strategy and assign preparation criteria. This should be based on his examination and study of the proposal, identified areas of customer concern, and backup data available. Each member of the team must understand the strategy and accept the goals. Common agreement should be reached regarding assigned roles and tactics.
- Check backup data for labor and material to be certain of their currency, correctness, adequacy, and completeness. Analyze weaknesses and strengths and make plans to downplay weaknesses and promote positions of strength.
- Prior to the negotiation conference, the lead negotiator should have an established negotiating position which has been agreed to by management. A negotiator must be given the limits of his authority concerning that particular negotiation, and he must have the authority to make decisions within those pre-established management boundaries. This involves all aspects of the submitted proposal, including the consideration of risks.
- The lead negotiator should instruct his team regarding their negotiating role in the forthcoming meeting. He should emphasize the need for total commitment to the company's goals and objectives.
- The lead negotiator should keep upper management advised of any significant risks that develop during the negotiations and obtain decisions regarding appropriate approaches and countermeasures.
- When an agreement is consummated, the lead negotiator should make certain that the customer has the germane information required to document the position attained during the course of negotiations and that all facets of the agreement as reached are understood by all parties. Agreements reached during the negotiations should be put in writing and endorsed by the participants.

Fig. 13.2 A negotiator's checklist.

contracts which provide for varying degrees of contractor cost responsibility. Matching of the type of contract to the specific job and conditions is one of the most important factors in successful negotiating. Factors that enter into the determination of contract type are listed in Figure 13.3. Under *Fixed Price* contracts, the company must produce

- Complexity of the item
- Stability of the design
- State of the art
- Specifications
- Prospective period of performance
- Adequacy of contractor's accounting system
- Contractor's technical capability and financial responsibility
- Urgency of the requirement
- Willingness of the contractor to assume risks

Fig. 13.3 Factors which determine the contract type.

the required items or perform the services for a firm fixed price or within the ceiling of an incentive contract. Under a *Cost Reimbursement* contract, the customer pays cost of material, labor, and a portion of overhead costs as provided for in the contract. These categories and types have many variations and are summarized below and in Figures 13.4 and 13.5.

Note that there are no absolute rules governing the selection of the appropriate contract type. Also, the contractor has the right to propose an alternative type than the one suggested in the RFP.

- *Firm Fixed Price (FFP).* The firm-fixed-price contract is the simplest and most widely used type of government contract. It is used where there is a reasonably definite design or performance specification. Basically, it involves only an agreement prior to the execution of the definitive contract on the price to be paid by the government for the products or services to be delivered by the contractor. Under this type of contract, the contractor assumes the maximum business risks and is provided with the maximum incentive to reduce development and production costs. Normally, fixed price procurements involve products or services for which

TYPE	CONTRACTOR COST RESPONSIBILITY	CONTRACTOR RISK
FFP	High	High
FPI	Some	Some
CPIF	Moderate	Moderate
CPFF	Least	Low

Fig. 13.4 Types of contracts versus contractor responsibilities and risks.

- Time and Materials Contracts.
- Letter Contracts.
- Basic Agreements.
- Basic Ordering Agreements.
- Facilities Contracts.
- Combination Contracts.

Fig. 13.5 Other types of contracts.

there is considerable competition, a standard design, prior manufacturing experience, and a fast delivery schedule. The government views the firm fixed price contract as "the most preferred
type" whenever costs are predictable withing a reasonable range
of accuracy.

Firm fixed price contracts account for eighty percent or more
of today's aerospace activities. The government's contract monitoring resources are largely geared to this kind of procurement,
including its several incentive variations.

- *Fixed Price with Escalation.* The fixed-price contract with escalation is the same as a firm-fixed-price contract except that the ultimate contract price may, as determined by the escalation provisions, be higher or lower than the original specified price. This
type of contract should be used in circumstances similar to those
calling for the use of a firm fixed price type contract except that
both parties agree that, for example, because of unstable wage
rates or fluctuating material costs a firm fixed price may not be
equitable.

- *Fixed Price With Redetermination.* A fixed-price with redetermination contract provides for a recalculation of the price after
a specified period. This type of contract reduces the contractor's
financial risk up to the point of redetermination after which the
contractor assumes the risk of a firm fixed price contract. The
government is phasing out the use of contracts with redetermination provisions.

- *Fixed Price Incentive (FPI).* A fixed-price-incentive contract provides for the revision of the target price through a formula for
the sharing of any difference between actual costs and the target
costs. The contractor is reimbursed for actual costs incurred plus
target profit adjusted upward or downward by a sharing formula
dependent upon whether the actual costs are less than or exceed
the original target costs.

This type of contract requires negotiation of (1) a target cost;
(2) a target profit; (3) a price ceiling — e.g., 110 percent of target
cost; and (4) a formula for government/contractor "sharing" of
cost overruns or underruns as determined by the target cost. A

profit ceiling or floor is not established and the contractor must bear all costs in excess of the price ceiling. A billing price is established as an interim basis for payment and may be adjusted, within ceiling limits, when it becomes apparent that actual costs will differ significantly from the target cost.

Fixed price incentive is used when less confidence exists than for a firm fixed price arrangement. It is also used to provide the contractor with a positive profit incentive to reduce costs.

- *Cost Plus Fixed Fee (CPFF).* A cost-plus-fixed-fee contract provides for payment of allowable costs incurred in the performance of the contract plus a predetermined fixed fee representing profit. The fee remains fixed regardless of the actual allowable costs unless the scope of the contract is increased or decreased. This type of contract is considered by the government to be suitable for use only when the uncertainties involved in contract performance are of such magnitude that cost of performance cannot be established with sufficient reasonableness to permit the use of any type of contract that would provide greater incentive to the contractor to control costs.

  Cost reimbursement contracts are scarce. When they occur, they're usually used for research and development type procurements whose uncertainties make accurate cost determination impractical. The contractor's downside risk is nonexistent, but profit is usually small or nonexistent also. Not so obvious though is the fact that cost reimbursement contracts can yield a high return on investment merely because investment can be quite small.

  In recent years, the government has discouraged the use of CPFF contracts on the premise that they provide the contractor with little motivation to reduce costs.

- *Cost Plus Incentive Fee (CPIF).* A cost-plus-incentive-fee contract is similar to the cost-plus-fixed-fee contract except that the fee is adjusted upward or downward based on the relationship of actual costs to target costs. Its use is most properly limited to those situations where ordinarily a cost-plus-fixed-fee contract would be used if there were greater certainty in the estimated costs.

Cost-plus-incentive-fee contracts require negotiation of a target cost, a target fee, a minimum and maximum fee, and a fee adjustment formula. They differ from fixed-price-incentive contracts in that price ceilings are not applicable and a profit (in the amount of the minimum fee) is assured.

* *Cost Plus Award Fee (CPAF).* A cost-plus-award-fee contract is a reimbursement contract with special fee provisions. These provide a means of establishing incentives in contracts which are not susceptible to finite measurements of performance as are necessary in incentive contracts. As in CPFF and CPIF contracts, CPAF contracts also provide for the recovery of acceptable costs. The fee, however, consists of two parts: (1) a fixed amount which does not vary with performance (called a "base fee") and (2) an award amount intended to provide motivation for excellence in contract performance in areas such as quality, timeliness, ingenuity, and cost effectiveness. Award fee may be earned in whole or in part; the amount of award fee to be paid is based on an evaluation by the government of the quality of the contractor's performance, judged in the light of criteria set forth in the contract.

   Contracts of this type include (1) a target cost; (2) a base fee commensurate with minimum acceptable performance; (3) criteria against which the contractor's performance will be evaluated; and (4) an additional fee, not to exceed a stipulated maximum, which is awarded on the basis of a subjective evaluation by the government of contractor performance. Determinations of the amount of award fee that has been earned (if any) are based on the reports of performance made by government personnel knowledgeable with respect to the contract requirements. Note that this is a unilateral determination made by the government, based on a subjective evaluation of the contractor's performance. The contractor does not have the right to protest the amount of award fee determined to have been earned.

* *Cost Without Fee.* A cost-without-fee contract provides for the recovery of acceptable costs only, and makes no provision for payment of fee or profit. Its major application is for the purchase of facilities used in connection with other government procurements.

- *Performance-Incentive.* A performance-incentive contract is generally a modified version of the fixed-price incentive or cost-plus-incentive contracts, and it provides for increases or decreases in profits based on performance factors in addition to cost performance. Examples of such factors are delivery, performance characteristics (computation rate, speed of a missile, ship, aircraft, thrust of an engine, fuel economy), technical accomplishments, overall management, and so on. Performance goals, measurement criteria, and the profit formula generally require considerable negotiation and subsequent administration.

- *Time and Material.* A time and material type contract provides for payment on the basis of direct labor hours at specified hourly rates (which rates include direct labor, overhead, and profit) and material at cost. This type of contract has some application for the procurement of supplies and/or services for repair, maintenance, or overhaul. Time and material contracts require considerable negotiation of the direct labor hour rate and have very limited usage.

- *Letter of Intent (Letter Contract).* A letter contract or letter of intent is a preliminary contract which is issued prior to the complete agreement between the government and contractor as to the definitive contract. This type of contract is used as an expediency to enable the initiation of production. Letter contracts and letters of intent subject the contractor to considerable financial risk due to the looseness of contractual terms and should be avoided wherever possible. When such agreements are accepted in situations which warrant their use, they should be converted to definitive agreements as soon as practicable.

Selection of the type of contract should not be based on the individual prejudices of either the government representative or the contractor's representative but rather on an objective analysis of all factors involved and the selection of the contract type that fits the particular procurement, all factors considered, including relative bargaining position.

14
How to Win International Contracts

- The role of export sales in your company's balance sheet.
- Offset, coproduction, and industrial participation contract's — What Are They?
- Resident agents — why you must have them.
- Foreign military sales — the approved channel.
- Export licenses — how to get them.
- National security.

Export sales can play a major role in the well-being of your company and the nation. Among the benefits that they can provide are the following.

- Pay for increasingly expensive oil imports.
- Reduce the country's trade deficits.
- Strengthen the dollar.
- Create additional jobs.
- Provide lower unit costs through volume manufacture.
- Eliminate the need for protectionist measures.

The last two decades have witnessed an unprecedented rise in U.S. trade with other countries. Export-related jobs have grown apace. But this growth has slowed sharply very recently, and some analysts, noting protectionist cries at home and abroad, fear a prolonged retrenchment in foreign trade.

This is somewhat surprising considering that international sales of products can do wonders for a company's balance sheet, helping to fill and smooth the valleys that otherwise occur when domestic business sours. But many small- to medium-size companies that are potential exporters face difficulty in tapping these large markets because they haven't a marketing structure capable of reaching these customers.

One solution is to market your product through a well-connected domestic organization that specializes in trade with foreign countries and operates on a commission basis. Another more direct approach is to develop your own international marketing capabilities. One place to start is the Department of Commerce. Its specialists can explain laws, customs, payment methods, arrange trade visits, and recommend other sources.

When marketing a product in a large number of Third World countries, it is often worthwhile to generate an unsolicited "generic" proposal that can be given to all, saving the costs for customized offerings.

Deciding which countries are likely prospects for your products and services can be made easier through a systematic assessment of each country's needs. Figure 14.1 is a checklist of items that should be

- General summary
- Population
- Capital
- Agents/Representatives
- Climate and topography
- Languages
- Travel information
  - Courtesies
  - Communications
  - Customs
  - Electric power standard
  - Laundry
  - Office services
  - Time zone
  - Water
  - Clothing
  - Airlines
  - Legal assistance
- Monetary standard
- Military assessment
  - Current military equipment
  - Military attaches
- Political assessment
  - Type of government
  - Procurement systems and process
- Balance of trade
  - Major Imports
  - Major Exports
- Current export licenses and their status
- Last Contact

Fig. 14.1 Checklist for a business intelligence dossier on a prospective foreign customer.

included in any comprehensive business intelligence assessment for a particular country. The completed checklist can facilitate initial contracts, proposal submittals, contract negotiations, and meetings during and after the contract period. The checklist can also provide valuable stimulants to conversation helping to overcome barriers to communication.

Export sales of aerospace and electronics industry products usually start with the dissemination of technical data, perhaps a sales proposal, either written or verbal. Before taking this step, however, you should first determine whether an export license is required. Licensing is centered primarily in the Departments of Commerce and State. The licensing procedure is depicted, generally, in the decision tree of Figure 14.2.

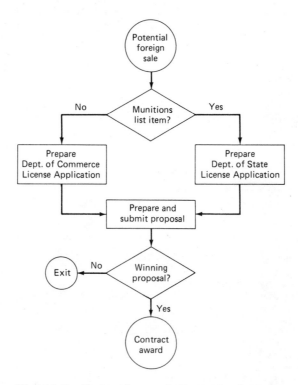

Fig. 14.2 Decision tree for pursuing international contracts.

The Department of Commerce has the broader jurisdiction whereas the Department of State regulates the export of defense articles including technical data, and defense services. Violation of export regulations, whether those of the Commerce or State Department can result in penalties such as suspension of export privileges or, in some cases, far more serious consequences.

In most countries it is desirable and often necessary to employ a local organization or individual to assist your company in soliciting business. This helps to ensure that each country's laws, policies, and customs are complied with. Foreign sales representation can be vital during the negotiation phases of international contracts. Local representation can also help bridge language barriers when they exist. In Saudi Arabia, for example, the Saudi government bars foreigners from selling goods in the country — except for some involving government purchases — so a Saudi citizen must be your sales agent or partner.

Offset, coproduction, or industrial participation contracts as they are sometimes called, are all collaborative arrangements in which the seller and buyer share the responsibilities and the benefits of successful contract performance. Offset can be an effective deal-closing strategy when marketing products in more advanced, industrialized countries. Technologically advanced countries sometimes *require* offset participation in many new business ventures. In recent examples, the part of the contract offset to the foreign participant typically runs 25 to 30 percent of the total contract value.

Joint ventures can provide the additional advantage that if protectionist measures are imposed, both parties may be able to continue doing business. Such defusing of protectionism is becoming increasingly significant.

When negotiating with foreign nationals, be aware of their particular characteristics. For example, Americans like to get things done right away. But Mexicans will take advantage of that. They will exhaust the Americans by moving things at a very slow pace. The Americans will lose patience and then give away more things in negotiation than they should have. It's a matter of understanding the culture.

Of growing concern is the requirement to conduct international business transactions without making unlawful payments, directly or indirectly. What are referred to, of course, are "kickbacks" or "bribes" intended to induce or reward favorable buying decisions or governmental actions.

DEPARTMENT OF COMMERCE

Licensing controls administered by the Department of Commerce provide for both general and specific (validated) licenses. General licenses provide for authorization of a number of items; validated licenses are used when a commodity requires individualized treatments.

It is important to determine whether a general or validated license is required for export of a particular commodity. The Commodity Control List issued by the Department of Commerce is the key to making this determination.

DEPARTMENT OF STATE

Export of aerospace products will more generally reside within the jurisdiction of the Department of State. These will fall into one of two categories: (1) Direct Foreign Sales which are typically commercial sales of products or services, and (2) Foreign Military Sales. Under the Foreign Military Sales procedure, the U.S. Government first buys the product for resale to the foreign customer.

To comply with export control laws, it is necessary to obtain a license to sell defense articles and defense services internationally. An export license is issued and controlled by the Department of State for items on the U.S. Munitions List. Export licensing regulations apply to technical data, both written and verbal, as well as to products and services in the conventional sense. Published data or other information which is in the public domain, such as catalogs and product brochures, are excluded.

When U.S. technology finds its way into Soviet weapons systems, the cost to the U.S. can far exceed the benefits in trade. And when international tensions become high, the government's reviewers of license applications will increase their vigilance. These reviewers must be alert to third party sales in which items having potential military application are sold to neutral countries, which then later end up in Soviet hands by means of retransfers. They must also be able to identify "dual-application" technology, such as certain types of computers, that although designed for innocuous purposes, can have important military uses as well. Guidance of modern missiles is one such possibility.

Despite these restrictions, the international sale of certain aerospace, electronic, and industrial products is, and will continue to be, an important source of revenue for many companies. This is especially true where any associated technology transfer has no effect on foreign military capabilities.

Here are a few strategy suggestions regarding Department of State export licenses: (1) When marketing a product in a number of countries, (in a recent count, there were 39 offices for procuring military equipment in the free world), try grouping the countries into collective regions, applying for export licenses covering the regions rather than individual countries. Administrative costs can be lowered substantially, both within your company and in the government. (2) No written technical material, unless previously released publicly, should be mailed or taken abroad, or given to a foreign national in the United States unless it has been determined that such data is covered by an existing license or is exempted from export license requirements. (3) When describing a commodity and its value on your license application, include support items (spare parts, maintenance documentation, computer programs, etc.). Otherwise, you may end up applying for three or four licenses where one would have been sufficient.

The Department of State regulates the export of all articles considered as arms, ammunition, implements of war, and technical data that relates to these items. It exercises this control through the application of its International Traffic In Arms Regulations, referred to simply as ITAR. ITAR, including its periodic amendments, is recommended reading for anyone expecting to become engaged in the export of these kinds of articles. ITAR will provide a current munitions list, critical definitions, licensing provisions and procedures, and other vital guidance. A company's marketing staff, technical staff, legal counsel, traffic manager, and contracts administrator may all eventually have a need to refer to the ITAR for variety of reasons.

Appendix A

**PROPOSAL WRITER'S DICTIONARY
OF ACRONYMS, INITIALISMS, AND ABBREVIATIONS**

AAA	Anti-Aircraft Artillery.
A/C	Aircraft.
AC	Alternating Current.
ACA	After Contract Award.
ACO	Administrative Contracting Officer.
ACWP	Actual Cost of Work Performed.
A/D CONVERTER	Analog to Digital Converter. A unit or device that converts an analog signal, that is, a signal in the form of a continuously variable voltage or current, to a digital signal.
ADP	Automatic Data Processing.
A&E	Architectural and Engineering.
AFLC	Air Force Logistics Command.
AFSC	Air Force Systems Command. Air Force command charged with development and acquisition of weapon systems/subsystems.
AGC	Automatic Gain Control.
AGE	Aerospace Ground Equipment.
AIAA	American Institute of Aeronautics and Astronautics.
ALU	Arithmetic-Logic Unit. The part of a CPU that executes adds, subtracts, shifts, AND logic operations, OR logic operations, etc.
ANT	Abstract of New Technology.
APR	Administrative Proposal Requirements.
AR	Army Regulation.
ARO	After Receipt of Order.
ASAP	As Soon As Possible.
ASCII	American Standard Code for Information Interchange. A standard code used extensively in data transmission, in which 128 numerals, letters, symbols, and special control codes are each represented by a 7-bit binary number (8 bits if a parity, or checking bit is added). For example, numer-

al 5 is represented by 011 0101, letter K by 100 1011, percent symbol (%) by 010 0101, and start of text (STX) control code by 00 0010.

ASD	Aeronautical Systems Division (Air Force Systems Command).
ASPR	Armed Services Procurement Regulations.
ATC	Air Training Command.
ATE	Automatic Test Equipment.
ATP	Acceptance Test Procedure.
AWG	American Wire Gauge.
BAFO	Best and Final Offer.
BASIC	Beginners All-Purpose Symbolic Instruction Code. A popular computer language, relatively easy to use.
BCD	Binary Coded Decimal. A coding system in which each decimal digit from 0 to 9 is represented by four binary digits (bits):

Decimal Digit	Binary Code	Decimal Digit	Binary Code
0	0000	5	0101
1	0001	6	0110
2	0010	7	0111
3	0011	8	1000
4	0100	9	1001

BCWP	Budgeted Cost of Work Performed.
BCWS	Budgeted Cost of Work Scheduled.
BIS	Board of Inspection and Survey.
BIT	Abbreviation for Binary Digit. A bit can have a value of either 0 or 1. In the BCD system, four bits represent one decimal digit.
BIT	Built-In-Test.
BITE	Built-In-Test Equipment.
BMEWS	Ballistic Missile Early Warning System.
BOA	Basic Ordering Agreement.
BTU	British Thermal Unit.
BWO	Backward Wave Oscillator.
BYTE	The number of bits that a computer processes as a unit. This may be equal to or less than the number of bits in a word. For example, both 8-bit and 16-bit word length computers process data in 8-bit bytes.

CA	Contract Award.
CAD	Computer-Aided Design.
CAI	Computer-Aided Instruction.
CBD	Commerce Business Daily.
CCB	Configuration Control Board.
C³I	Command, Control, Communication, and Intelligence.
CCD	Charge Coupled Device. A semiconductor storage device in which an electrical charge is moved across the surface of a semiconductor by electrical control signals. Zeroes or ones are represented by the absence or presence of a charge.
CCTV	Closed Circuit Television.
CD	Calendar Days.
CDR	Critical Design Review. A formal meeting between government and contractor representatives at which the system process is reviewed and a formal risk assessment in time, cost, and technical difficulty is presented. Successful completion of CDR signifies the completion of the basic design.
CDRL	Contract Data Requirements List.
CEI	Contract End Item.
CFE	Contractor-Furnished Equipment.
CFSR	Contract Funds Status Report.
CI	Contractor Inquiry. A formal request for clarification of an item in a contractor's proposal.
CI	Configuration Item. An aggregation of hardware/computer programs or any of its discrete portions, which satisfies an end-use function and is designated for configuration management.
C.I.E.	Commission Internationale de l'Eclairage.
CLI	Contract Line Item.
CLIN	Contract Line Item Number.
CLS	Contractor Logistics Support.
CM	Configuration Management.
CMOS	Complementary Metal-Oxide-Semiconductor. Although strictly speaking, CMOS refers to an IC manufacturing technology, the term is almost always used to describe an IC logic family. The CMOS logic family is characterized by very low power dissipation, low circuit density per chip, and moderate speed of operation when compared to other IC logic families. (See ECL, TTL, and I^2L)
CMP	Configuration Management Plan.
CNO	Chief of Naval Operations.

CO	Contracting Officer.
COM	Computer Output Microfilm.
CONUS	Continental United States.
COTR	Contracting Officer's Technical Representative.
CPAF	Cost Plus Award Fee. Contractor's variable fee is determined subjectively on the basis of periodic after-the-fact evaluation of contractor's performance. (Operations, technical or business management, utilization of resources, etc.) Base fee may be zero.
CPCI	Computer Program Configuration Item.
CPFF	Cost Plus Fixed Fee. A cost reimbursement type contract which provides for the payment of a fixed fee to the contractor. The fixed fee, once negotiated, does not vary with actual cost, but may be adjusted as a result of any subsequent changes in the scope of work or services to be performed under the contract.
CPIF	Cost Plus Incentive Fee. A cost reimbursement type contract which provides for a fee adjusted by a formula relating actual allowed cost to target cost.
CPM	Cost Performance Measurement.
CPR	Cost Performance Report or Cost Proposal Requirements.
CPS	Computer Program System.
CPU	Central Processing Unit. That part of a computer system that controls the interpretation and execution of instructions. In general the CPU contains the following elements: arithmetic logic unit (ALU); timing and control; accumulator; scratch pad memory; program counter and address stack; instruction register and I/O.
CRO	Cathode-Ray Oscilloscope.
CRT	Cathode-Ray Tube. A unit or device, similar to a television picture tube, which provides a visual, nonpermanent display of system input/output data, such as instructions as they are being developed and data in storage.
C/SCSC	Cost/Schedule Control System Criteria. A major administrative and reporting system involving a formal government evaluation of cost compliance.
C/SPCS	Cost/Schedule Planning and Control System.
C/SSR	Cost/Schedule Status Report. A formal reporting system prepared by contractors to provide summarized cost and schedule performance information for program management purposes.

CW	Continuous Wave.
CWBS	Contract Work Breakdown Structure.
CY	Calendar Year.

DA	Department of the Army.
D/A CONVERTER	Digital-to-Analog Converter. A unit or device that converts a digital signal into a voltage or current whose magnitude is proportional to the numeric value of the digital signal. For example, see table:

Digital Input	Analog Output (volts)
00101 (binary 5)	2
01010 (binary 10)	4
10100 (binary 20)	8

DAC	Days After Contract.
DAR	Defense Acquisition Regulation.
DARCOM	Development and Readiness Commands. U.S. Army command charged with development, acquisition, and logistics support functions.
DARPA	Defense Advanced Research Projects Agency.
DARS	Defense Acquisition Regulatory System.
DBMS	Data Base Management System.
DC	Direct Current.
DCAA	Defense Contracts Audit Agency. An independent agency within the Department of Defense which provides contract audit services to federal agencies.
DCAS	Defense Contracts Administration Services.
DCASO	Defense Contracts Administration Services Office.
DCASR	Defense Contracts Administration Services Region.
DDC	Defense Documentation Center.
DDRE	Director of Defense Research and Engineering.
DIA	Defense Intelligence Agency.
DID	Data Items Description.
DIP	Dual In-Line Package. A package for electronic components that is suited for automated assembly into printed circuit boards. The DIP is characterized by two rows of external connecting terminals, or pins, which are inserted into the holes of the printed circuit board.
DIS	Data Item Specification.

DMA	Defense Mapping Agency.
DMA	Direct Memory Access. A mechanism that allows an input/output device to take control of the CPU for one or more memory cycles in order to write into memory or read from memory. The order of executing the program steps (instructions) remains unchanged.
DOD	Department of Defense.
DODI	Department of Defense Instruction.
DODISS	Department of Defense Index of Specifications and Standards.
DOE	Department of Energy.
DOS	Disk Operating System. A collection of programs which facilitate use of a disk drive.
DR	Discrepancy Report.
DSARC	Defense System Acquisition Review Committee.
DTC	Design to Cost.
DTL	Diode-Transistor Logic. A now little-used form of semiconductor logic, having been replaced largely by TTL.
DTUPC	Design to Unit Production Cost.
EAROM	Electrically-Alterable Read-Only Memory. A ROM that can be erased and reprogrammed any number of times.
ECL	Emitter-Coupled Logic. An IC logic family characterized by its very high speed of operation, low circuit density per chip and very high power dissipation when compared to other IC logic families. (See *CMOS, TTL, I^2L*).
ECN	Engineering Change Notice.
ECP	Engineering Change Proposal.
EDP	Electronic Data Processing.
EDR	Engineering Design Review. A formal meeting between government and contractor representatives to provide information, answer questions, clarify requirements and serve as a review of performance and other engineering related matters.
EIA	Electronic Industries Association.
EMC	Electromagnetic Compatibility.
EMI	Electromagnetic Interference.
EPA	Environmental Protection Agency.
EPROM	Erasable Programmable Read-Only Memory. A form of ROM, the contents of which can be set by the user.
ERU	Equipment Replacement Unit.

EUR	Europe.
EW	Electronic Warfare.
FCA	Functional Configuration Audit.
FET	Field-Effect Transistor. A transistor whose internal operation is unipolar in nature. The metal-oxide semiconductor FET (MOSFET) is widely used in IC's because the devices are very small and can be manufactured with few steps.
FFP	Firm Fixed Price contract. A type of contract which generally provides for a firm price, or under appropriate circumstances may provide for an adjustable price, for the supplies or services which are being procured.
FIFO	First In, First Out. The way certain kinds of computer memory operates. Analogous to the way a checkout stand at a supermarket works.
FMS	Foreign Military Sales. A U.S. Government program to control the export of equipment to the armed forces of foreign countries. Under the FMS program, the U.S. Government first buys the product for subsequent resale to the foreign customer.
F/O	Follow-On.
FOIA	Freedom of Information Act.
FORTRAN	Formula Translator. A programming language designed for problems which can be expressed in algebraic notation allowing for exponentiation and up to three subscripts. The FORTRAN compiler is a routine for a given machine which accepts a program written in FORTRAN source language and produces a machine language routine object program. FORTRAN II added considerably to the power of the original language by giving it the ability to define and use almost unlimited hierarchies of subroutines, all sharing a common storage region if desired. Later improvements have added the ability to use Boolean expressions, and some capabilities for inserting symbolic machine language sequences within a source program.
FPI	Fixed Price Incentive. Type of contract with provision for the adjustment of profit and price by a formula based on the relationship which final negotiated total cost bears to negotiated target cost as adjusted by approved changes.
FPLA	Field Programmable Logic Array.
FQR	Formal Qualification Review.

FSD	Full Scale Development.
FSED	Full Scale Engineering Development.
FUD	Fear, Uncertainty, and Doubt. A computer industry euphemism.
FY	Fiscal Year. A twelve-month period selected for accounting purposes. The federal fiscal year begins on 1 October of each year and ends on 30 September of the following year.
G&A	General and Administrative (expense).
Gantt Chart	A bargraph depicting work planned or completed in relation to time.
GAO	General Accounting Office.
GFE	Government-Furnished Equipment.
GFP	Government-Furnished Property.
GLP	Government-Loaned Property.
GO	Graphic Oriented (Proposal Preparation Technique).
GSA	General Services Administration.
HBK	Handbook.
HEW	Health, Education, and Welfare.
HSI	Hardware, Software Integration.
HUD	Housing and Urban Development.
IAW	In Accordance With. Popular RFP phrase often applied without definition.
IC	Integrated Circuit. A very small electronic device containing a silicon chip on which hundreds to thousands of electronic components are fabricated. This is a monolithic IC, as opposed to a hybrid IC. Sometimes the chip itself is referred to as an IC, but strictly speaking an IC is the packaged chip with leads from the chip brought out through the package.
ICBM	Intercontinental Ballistic Missile.
ICD	Interface Control Document.
IEEE	Institute of Electrical and Electronic Engineers.
IFB	Invitation for Bid. Advertised request to submit a sealed bid. Contract awarded to lowest responsible offeror.
I^2L	Integrated Injection Logic. The newest of the logic families, which to an extent combines bipolar speed, MOS circuit density, and the low power dissipation of CMOS.

ILS	Integrated Logistics Support. A composite of all "after sale" activities which contribute to the continuing operation of a system.
ILSP	Integrated Logistics Support Plan.
I/O	Input-Output. A general term for the equipment used to communicate with a computer and the data involved in the communication.
IOC	Initial Operating Capability.
IOT&E	Initial Operational Test and Evaluation.
IPE	Industrial Plant Equipment.
IR	Infrared.
IR&D	Independent Research and Development. That internal research and/or development that is not covered by a contract or grant.
ISD	Instructional System Development.
ITAR	International Traffic in Arms Regulations.
ITP	Instruction To Proceed.
JAN	Joint Army-Navy (Specification).
K	1000 or 1024 words.
KB	Kilobytes.
LASER	Light Amplification by Stimulated Emission of Radiation.
LCC	Life Cycle Costs.
LCD	Liquid Crystal Display. A multisegment display device consisting basically of a liquid crystal hermetically sealed between two glass plates. One type of LCD depends upon a backlighting source. The readout is either dark characters on a dull white background or white on a dull black background. LCD's have very low power requirements.
LED	Light Emitting Diode. A semiconductor device that gives off light when current passes through it. LED's are constructed in either a multisegment display format or a dot matrix display format. Red, orange, green, and yellow readouts are produced, but red is used most often because of its lower cost.
LIFO	Last In, First Out.
LOE	Level Of Effort.
LRU	Line Replaceable Unit.
LSA	Logistics Support Analysis.

LSAR	Logistics Support Analysis Record
LSB	Least Significant Bit.
LSC	Logistics Support Costs.
LSI	Large Scale Integration. Monolithic IC's of very high density. Such circuits typically have on a single chip the equivalent of more than 100 simple logic circuits.
MAC	Months After Contract.
MIL-SPEC	Military Specification
MIL-STD	Military Standard.
MODEM	Modulator-Demodulator. An electronic device that modulates and demodulates signals transmitted over communications lines. For example, the digital output of a microprocessor might be modulated to form a frequency-modulated signal (analog) for easier transmission over communications lines. Conversely, the modem would demodulate a frequency-modulated signal to change it back to a digital signal.
MOS	Metal-Oxide-Semiconductor. A semiconductor manufacturing technology used to produce IC logic components. MOS devices are unipolar, as compared with bipolar devices. The term "unipolar" is seldom used; MOS, which implies "unipolar" is often used in its place. For example, "MOS devices are slower than bipolar devices."
MOSFET	Metal-Oxide-Semiconductor Field Effect Transistor. (See *MOS*.)
MOU	Memorandum of Understanding.
MR	Modification Request.
MSB	Most Significant Bit.
MSI	Medium-Scale Integration. Monolithic IC's of intermediate density. Such circuits typically have on a single chip the equivalent of 50 to 100 simple logic circuits.
MTBD	Mean-Time-Between-Devices. That period of time from the installation of an item in a single application to its failure/ removal and replacement.
MTBF	Mean-Time-Between-Failures. The MTBF for a particular piece of equipment in a given time interval is the mean value of the operating periods between all failures occuring in that equipment during that interval.
MTTR	Mean-Time-To-Repair.

NASA	National Aeronautics and Space Administration.
NATC	Naval Aviation Training Command.
NAVMAT	Naval Material Command. U.S. Navy command dedicated to the System Acquisition Process.
NBS	National Bureau of Standards.
NC	Numerical Control. The technique of controlling a machine or process through the use of command instructions in coded numerical form.
NEMA	National Electrical Manufacturers' Association.
NFO	Naval Flight Officer.
NLT	Not Later Than.
NOFORN	No Foreign Dissemination.
NPE	Navy Preliminary Evaluator.
NRZ	Nonreturn to Zero.
NRZI	Nonreturn to Zero Inverted.
NTE	Navy Technical Evaluator.
NTEC	Naval Training Equipment Center. Procures training equipment on behalf of all four services.
NTSC	National Television Standards Committee.
OCONUS	Outside the Continental United States (Overseas)
OCR	Optical Character Recognition.
OEM	Original Equipment Market.
OFPP	Office of Federal Procurement Policy.
OHA	Operating Hazard Analysis.
O&M	Operation and Maintenance.
OMB	Office of Management and Budgets.
OP AMP	Operational Amplifier. An exceptionally versatile linear amplifier (usually a linear IC) used extensively in control, computation, and measurement applications.
ORLA	Optimum Repair Level Analysis.
OT&E	Operational Test and Evaluation.
PCA	Physical Configuration Audit.
PCB	Printed Circuit Board.
PCM	Pulse Code Modulation.
PCO	Procuring Contracting Officer.
PD	Preliminary Design.
PDR	Preliminary Design Review. A formal meeting between government and contractor representatives at which the contractor presents his basic design approach for a configuration item.

PDS	Program Design Specification.
PEL	Picture Element.
PERT	Program Evaluation and Review Technique. A network-type planning and control tool for modern management. Developed during the late 1950's, PERT became famous after successful application to the Navy's Polaris Program. During the 1960's, PERT and related techniques gained popularity throughout industry and government. Today PERT is a widely used management tool. Many contracts and budget proposals require a PERT chart documentation.
pH	A number used for expressing the acidity or alkalinity of solutions. A value of 7 is natural in a scale ranging from 0 to 14. Solutions lower than 7 are considered acid while those higher are alkaline.
PHA	Preliminary Hazard Analysis.
PHL	Preliminary Hazard List.
PHR	Preliminary Hazard Review.
PIDS	Prime Item Development Specification.
PIXEL	Picture Element.
PLA	Programmable Logic Array. A general-purpose logic structure consisting of an array of logic circuits. The way in which these circuits are programmed determines how input signals to the PLA are processed. Programming is done on a custom basis at the factory and permanently establishes the functional operation of the PLA.
PM	Program Manager.
PMD	Program Management Directive. Document that provides guidance for initiating a program.
PMR	Program Management Review. A formal communication of the status of a program and the vehicle wherein management concerns are addressed.
PPS	Program Performance Specification.
PR	Purchase Request.
PROM	Programmable ROM. A ROM that can be programmed by the user, but only once. After a PROM is programmed, effectively it becomes a ROM.
PWB	Printed Wiring Board.
QA	Quality Assurance.
QC	Quality Control.

RAM	Random Access Memory. As most commonly defined, a RAM is a read/write memory. A more strict definition of a RAM is a memory that stores information in such a way that each bit of information may be retrieved within the same amount of time as any other bit. (As opposed to serial memory.)
RCC	Revision Collection Copy.
R&D	Research and Development.
RDT&E	Research, Development, Test, and Evaluation.
RF	Radio Frequency.
RFP	Request for Proposals. The documents used to invite proposals for supplies or services.
RFQ	Request for Quote. An inquiry which usually does not require a proposal. Evaluation is by price comparison alone if the bidder unconditionally accepts all the responsibilities, terms, and conditions as set forth in the inquiry.
RFTP	Request For Technical Proposal.
R/M	Reliability/Maintainability.
ROC	Required Operational Capability. Document that establishes a need, outlines existing deficiencies, describes an operational concept, and sets performance parameters.
ROI	Return On Investment.
ROM	Read-Only Memory. A memory in which information is stored permanently, e.g., a math function or a microprogram. A ROM is programmed according to the user's requirements during memory fabrication and cannot be reprogrammed.
ROM	Rough Order of Magnitude.
RPSTL	Repair Parts and Special Tools List.
RTL	Resistor-Transistor Logic. One of the earliest forms of semiconductor logic in which the basic logic element is a resistor-transistor network. RTL is now little used.
SAM	Surface-to-Air Missile.
SAMSO	Space and Missile Systems Organization (Air Force Systems Command).
SCCB	Software Configuration Control Board.
SCMP	Software Configuration Management Plan.
SCN	Specification Change Notice.
SCP	Software Change Proposal.

SCR	Silicon-Controlled Rectifier. A semiconductor device that functions as an electrically controlled switch for loads. The SCR is one type of thyristor.
SDR	System Design Review.
SEC	Source Evaluation Committee.
SEM	Standard Electronic Module.
SEMP	System Engineering Management Plan.
SHA	System Hazard Analysis.
S/N	Signal-to-Noise Ratio.
SOW	Statement of Work. The SOW is a description of the tasks, products, and/or services to be procured.
SPEC	Specification. A document which states what products must do.
SPO	System Program Office (Air Force). A dedicated group of project personnel responsible for managing the procurement of a system.
SPTE	Special Purpose Test Equipment.
SRR	System Requirements Review.
SSA	Source Selection Authority.
SSAC	Source Selection Advisory Council.
SSC	Source Selection Committee.
SSEB	Source Selection Evaluation Board.
SSI	Small Scale Integration. Less than 50 gates per chip.
SSPP	System Safety Program Plan.
STAR	Scientific and Technical Aerospace Reports. *NASA* information service.
STINFO	Scientific and Technical Information.
STOP	Sequential Thematic Organization of Publications. An ordered, structured format and procedure for preparing complex engineering and scientific documentation.
S/V	Survivability/Vulnerability.
SWR	Standing Wave Ratio.
SWWBS	Software Work Breakdown Structure.
TAWC	Tactical Air Warfare Center. (U.S. Air Force, Eglin AFB, FL).
TBD	To Be Determined.
TCP	Task Change Proposal.
TCP	Technical Change Proposal.
TCTO	Time Compliance Technical Order.

TDP	Technical Data Package.
T&E	Test and Evaluation.
TLU	Table Look-Up.
T&M	Time and Materials.
TMP	Technical Manual Plan.
TO	Technical Order.
TP	Test Plan.
TPM	Technical Performance Measurement.
TPR	Technical Proposal Requirements. A document stating the required format and content of an offeror's technical proposal.
TPSAA	Test, Pack, Ship, Assembly, and Acceptance.
TTL or T^2L	Transistor-Transistor Logic. Presently the most widely used form of semiconductor logic. Its basic logic element is a multiple-emitter transistor. TTL is characterized by fairly high speed and medium power dissipation.
TTY	Teletypewriter.
TV	Television.
UHF	Ultra High Frequency, 300,000 to 3,000,000 kilohertz.
USAREUR	United States Army, Europe.
UV	Ultraviolet.
VCO	Voltage Controlled Oscillator.
VE	Value Engineering.
VECP	Value Engineering Change Proposal.
VEP	Value Engineering Program.
VHF	Very High Frequency. 30,000 to 300,000 kilohertz.
VHSIC	Very High-Speed Integrated Circuit.
VLSI	Very Large Scale Integration. Integrated circuits containing some 100,000 simple logic circuits and transistors.
VSWR	Voltage Standing Wave Ratio.
WAG	Wild-Assed Guess. An aerospace industry euphemism.
WBS	Work Breakdown Structure. A product-oriented family tree composed of hardware, software, services, and other work tasks which organizes, defines, and graphically displays the product to be produced as well as the work to be accomplished in order to achieve the specified product.
XMTR	Transmitter.
ZBB	Zero Based Budgeting. A budgeting technique, now past its heyday, in which only absolutely essential items make up the budget baseline.

Appendix B

Mark	Meaning	Mark	Meaning
∧	Insert material here	∧ (comma)	Insert comma
stet	Retain crossed-out material	⊙	Insert period
....	Retain words under which dots appear	∧ (semicolon)	Insert semicolon
≡	Capitalize	/?/	Insert question mark
◯	Close up; no space	/!/	Insert exclamation mark
no ¶	No paragraph	(–)	Insert hyphen
¶	Paragraph	(/)	Insert parenthesis
⌐⌐	Transpose words or characters	∨	Insert apostrophe
ℓ	Delete	∨ ∨	Insert quotation marks
ℓ (circled)	Delete and close up	∨b	Insert superscript letter
#	Insert space	∧9	Insert subscript numeral
[	Move this to left	∅	Make lower case
]	Move this to right	⌐*out*⌐	Something omitted. See copy for material and insert here
sp	Spell out (or: typist, check spelling)	*caps*	Capital letters
l.c.	Lower case	*s.c.*	Small capitals

*These markings deviate somewhat from "Proofreader's Marks" because the proposal editor communicates with a typist instead of a typesetter.

Appendix C

LATIN REFERENCE TERMS

ca. (*circa*)	about
et al. (*et alii*)	and others
etc. (*et cetera*)	and so forth
e.g. (*exempli gratia*)	for example
et seq. (*et sequens*)	and the following
ibid. (*ibidem*)	in the same place
i.e. (*id est*)	that is
loc. cit. (*loco citato*)	in the place cited
op. cit. (*opere citato*)	in the work cited
sic (spell out)	thus
viz. (*videlicet*)	namely
vs. (*versus*)	against
q.e.d (*quad erat demonstrandum*)	which was to be shown

Appendix D

TWO-LETTER STATE ABBREVIATIONS

Alabama	AL		Montana	MT
Alaska	AK		Nebraska	NE
Arizona	AZ		Nevada	NV
Arkansas	AR		New Hampshire	NH
California	CA		New Jersey	NJ
Canal Zone	CZ		New Mexico	NM
Colorado	CO		New York	NY
Connecticut	CT		North Carolina	NC
Delaware	DE		North Dakota	ND
District of Columbia	DC		Ohio	OH
Florida	FL		Oklahoma	OK
Georgia	GA		Oregon	OR
Guam	GM		Pennsylvania	PA
Hawaii	HI		Puerto Rico	PR
Idaho	ID		Rhode Island	RI
Illinois	IL		South Carolina	SC
Indiana	IN		South Dakota	SD
Iowa	IA		Tennessee	TN
Kansas	KS		Texas	TX
Kentucky	KY		Utah	UT
Louisiana	LA		Vermont	VT
Maine	ME		Virginia	VA
Maryland	MD		Virgin Islands	VI
Massachusetts	MA		Washington	WA
Michigan	MI		West Virginia	WV
Minnesota	MN		Wisconsin	WI
Mississippi	MS		Wyoming	WY
Missouri	MO			

Appendix E

A FEW "GOOD WRITING" REFERENCES

1. Air Force Pamphlet 13-2, *Guide for Air Force Writing,* Dept. of the Air Force, 1973, Headquarters U.S. Air Force, Washington, D.C. 20330.
2. Hoover, H. H., *Essentials for the Scientific and Technical Writer,* Dover Press.
3. Strunk, William J., and White, E. B., *The Elements of Style,* The MacMillan/ Company, 1972.
4. Trimble, John R., *Writing With Style,* Prentice-Hall, Inc. 1975.
5. The University of Chicago Press, *A Manual of Style,* rev. 13th ed., Chicago: The University of Chicago Press, 1982.
6. *U.S. Government Printing Office Style Manual,* Superintendent of Documents, U.S. Government Printing Office, Washington, D.C. 10402.

Index

best and final offer, 99
bid set, 34
bidders' briefing, 33
billing milestones, 83
binding, 125-126
boilerplate, 6, 37, 72
bottom-up estimating, 96
briefings, 31-34
brochures, 155-157
business plan, 16-22
business intelligence, 23-29
 sources, 25-27
 strategies, 24
business plan, 16-22
 generalized example of, 18
 goals of, 19-20
 strategies for, 19

clarification requests. *see* contractor
 inquiries.
Commerce Business Daily, 37
competitive range, 160
configuration management, 93-94
consultants, 78-80
contract types, 163-169
 cost plus award fee, 168
 cost plus fixed fee, 165, 167
 cost plus incentive fee, 165, 167
 cost without fee, 168
 firm fixed price, 163-165
 fixed price incentive, 165-166
 fixed price with escalation, 166
 fixed price with redetermination, 166
 letter of intent (letter contract), 169
 performance-incentive, 169
 time and material, 169
contractor inquiries, 149-150
coproduction. *see* offset.
cost volume, 95-105
cover, 135-137
cover letter, 14, 105, 137-140

cross-reference index, 119
customer engineering/field services, 90-91

debriefings, 151
Delphi (method for developing a technical
 solution), 68
design review, 100

editing, 112-125
engineering review, 104
executive summary, 57-61
experience background, 71, 83-86
export licenses, 172-175
 Department of Commerce, 174
 Department of State, 174-175

facilities and equipment, 71, 80-81, 91
fly-off competitions, 36
foreign military sales, 174
four-step advertised procurements, 35-36
Freedom of Information Act, 24-28

Gantt Chart, 83, 127
goldplating, 64, 111
government furnished equipment, 40
group editing, 121

illustrations, 126-133
industrial participation. *see* offset.
integrated logistics support. *see* logistics
 support volume.
international contracts, 170-175
International Traffic in Arms Regulations,
 175
invitations for bids, 34

kickoff meeting, 14, 50-51

life cycle costs, 71, 88
logistics support volume, 71, 87-94
logotype, 130

maintainability, 40
management control system, 73
management plan, 75–77
management review, 105
management volume, 70–86
matrix organizational structure, 74–75
mean-time-between-failures, 93
mean-time-to-repair, 93
motherhood, 58, 92–93

negotiated procurements, 35
negotiations, 160–169
    "divide and conquer" strategem, 163
    "lowballing," 162
    "missing man" technique, 162
    "opening gun discomposer," 163
    "silence can be golden" gambit, 162
network diagram, 81–83
news releases, 157–159

offset, 173
operation and maintenance training, 89–90
optical character recognition, 119
order effect, 144–145
pasteup, 141
PERT chart, 102, 127
postproposal effort, 143–159
preproposal effort, 30–49
presentations, 151–155
    visual aids for, 153–155
press releases. see news releases.
pricing, 104–105
printing, 140–141
probability of award, 44–45
probability of funding, 44–45
profit, 104–105
program organization, 71, 74–75, 80
project organizational structure, 74–75
proposal
    alternate, 41
    cost of, 5, 42–46
    deficiencies of, 111
    definition of, 2
    delivery of, 142
    duration of, 7, 13, 14
    evaluation of, 144–149
    features of, 3–5, 141
    management of, 6–9
    page limits of, 135
    preparation procedure/schedule, 9–14
    staffing, 5–6, 9

unsolicited, 33, 41–42
proprietary legends, 17, 27–28, 138, 150

red team, 10, 106–111
related experience. see experience background.
reliability, 40
reliability and maintainability, 92–93
request for proposal, 2, 14, 21, 30–41, 47, 51, 144–146
request for proposals, 2, 7–8, 21, 30–35, 37, 40, 41, 47, 62, 63, 106–107, 109–111, 144–147
resumes, 77–79
reverse engineering, 28–29
revision collection cycle/copy, 10–12, 121–122
risk assessment, 19–22

schedule, 71, 81–83, 130–131
scoring, 145–149
shall versus will, 40–41
sidebar, 123–125
sole-source procurements, 34–35
spare and repair parts, 90
spread sheets, 95, 104–105
staffing plan, 71
statement of problem, 65–66
statement of work, 37, 39, 67
storyboarding, 51–57
strawman proposal, 32–33
summary and introduction, 64–65
system engineering management plan, 72

technical discussion (of approaches), 66–69
technical proposal requirements. see proposal preparation instructions.
technical publications, 91–92
technical volume, 62–69
thematic titling, 123
themes, 32, 52, 58, 59, 124, 137
title page, 136–138
top-down estimating, 96
trade shows, 158
transmittal letter. see cover letter.
two-step advertised procurements, 35
typography plan, 133–134

word processing, 119–120
work breakdown structure, 73, 100–102
work packages, 73, 101–102